"*The Public Orphanage* is a fresh and accurate critique of America's educational system. Free of the murky jargon of educators and policy wonks, the book reveals where the current direction of our public school system is taking us: ineffective and moral illiterates. Eric Buehrer not only describes where we are headed, but he provides concrete suggestions to redirect our schools and reclaim their traditional mission."

—**Dr. Kevin Ryan, Boston University, School of Education**

"It completely gripped me! I couldn't put it down. The Pied Piper of public education is merrily leading America's children into the dark cave of oblivion from which few will emerge. *The Public Orphanage* compellingly warns of the relentless advance of a terrible doom. America must respond in order to salvage a generation and save our future. Thank you, Buehrer!"

—**Rabbi Daniel Lapin, President, Toward Tradition**

"With *The Public Orphanage*, Eric Buehrer confronts directly the fundamental question underlying all family policy: Who shall raise the next generation—parents or the government? Buehrer's diagnosis of the problem is right on target, and his prescriptions for reform offer a ray of hope for the American family."

—**Greg D. Erkin, Executive Director, Of the People**

"In his timely book, Mr. Buehrer reveals our true education problem: we have allowed the so-called "experts" to take too much responsibility for our children. In the Gingrichian era of devolution, it is not enough to simply transfer authority back to state and local authorities. As Buehrer points out, the real revolution will only occur when parents reclaim the power over children from the "experts." Hopefully, liberals and conservatives alike will benefit from Buehrer's contention that the answers to our education problems will be found not in Washington or our state capitals, but in our own living rooms."

—**William F. Lauber, Research Associate, Heritage Foundation**

"*The Public Orphanage* delineates the fragmenting effects of the specialization of education and its gradual and eventual rejection of the traditional values of most parents. Eric Buehrer clearly and descriptively lays out the case against this specialization, particularly when married to missionary and radical relativism, an agenda not only of displacing the family but undermining it. Buehrer instead outlines how public schools can again become domains of cooperation between parents and teachers who want to preserve the public school system from the radicals who will eventually destroy it."

—**Patrick Fagan, Senior Policy Analyst, The Heritage Foundation**

"Eric Buehrer has performed a great service for this nation in his studies, his research, his observations, and his conclusions in *The Public Orphanage* which informs the reader of the truth regarding so many of our public schools. He does not cloak his writing in diplomatic jargon, which is done so often in contemporary writing on controversial topics. Instead, Eric Buehrer presents his immense knowledge in a book in which the reader becomes an integral part. *The Public Orphanage* may well get the reader angry, but such anger is justified—and Eric Buehrer's recommendations, if enacted will change the nation for the better."

—**Bruce Herschensohn, Senior Fellow, The Claremont Institute**

THE PUBLIC ORPHANAGE

ERIC BUEHRER

WORD PUBLISHING
Dallas·London·Vancouver·Melbourne

THE PUBLIC ORPHANAGE

Library of Congress Cataloging-in-Publication Data

Buehrer, Eric.
　　　The public orphanage : how public schools are making parents irrelevant /
Eric Buehrer.
　　　　　　　p. cm.
　　　Includes bibliographical references and index.
　　　ISBN 0-8499-3532-6
　　　1. Public schools—United States. 2. Education—United States—Aims and
objectives. 3. Home and school—United States.
　　　I. Title.
LA217.2.B82 1995　　　　　　　　　　　　　　　　　　　　95-1987
371'.01'0973–dc20　　　　　　　　　　　　　　　　　　　　CIP

Printed in the United States of America
5 6 7 8 9 RRD 9 8 7 6 5 4 3 2 1

To my brother, Dick.

Contents

Acknowledgements

I have to extend a special thanks to two people who made the idea for writing this book a reality. First, I thank my brother, Dr. Richard Buehrer, who spent hours and hours discussing, debating, reviewing, and refining my thoughts on the subject. He is a superb thinker and gave an eloquence to my views that raised my final draft to a higher level than it could have reached without him. Dick, your insights are magnificent.

Second, I thank Michael Flanagan for providing me an office where I wrote this book. Not only did he graciously provide me an office and all the furnishings I needed, he gave me much moral support and encouragement along the way. Mike, your generosity is a blessing.

I also want to thank Joey Paul and Laura Kendall of Word Publishing for sticking with me during the two years it took to write this book. Joey, your belief in the project meant a lot to me. Laura, your editorial insights helped me craft a better book.

Finally, I thank my wife, Kim, for her patience and support while I obsessed about the concepts and research for this project. Honey, how about we finally take that weekend getaway I promised?

Part One
From School to Orphanage

The general shape of the demand for a new institution is clear: It is a demand not for further classroom activities, not for further classroom indoctrination, nor for any particular content, but a demand for child care. It is a demand for care, first, all day from birth to school age; second, after school every day until parents return from work; and, third, all summer.

James Coleman, sociologist

R ECENTLY, PEOPLE HAVE BEEN shocked that House Speaker Newt Gingrich would resurrect the word *orphanage* and thrust it into the public vocabulary. The irony is that many of the people whose sensibilities are so offended by talk of public orphanages are enthusiastically supportive of expanding the role of public schools to become part-time versions of just such institutions.

The difference between a school and an orphanage is that a school's mission is to teach children while an orphanage's job is to care for them. As America's social ills mount, we have turned to our public schools for salvation. We have expanded the schools' mission in an attempt to solve our problems. In the name of *helping* parents we have, in essence, asked schools to *replace* them.

The president of the University of Southern California, Steven Sample, recently observed,

> We use our [elementary and secondary] schools as political mechanisms to achieve all kinds of social and political goals. We use them as police. We have dismantled the family in America in a way that no other industrial society has, so now we want our schools to be surrogate families, physicians, priests,

parents. We want them to be agents of social change, to solve our racial problems. So the schools cannot do their job of teaching English and mathematics, the main job of elementary and secondary schools.[1]

What Sample is describing is a new type of public orphanage—an institution for the care of abandoned children—but we call it a public school.

With a matter-of-fact tone (and a hint of satisfaction) policymakers tell us that the days of the Ozzie-and-Harriet family are over. Rather than strategize on how they can help us get those days back, they tell us how government employees will be the new Ozzies and Harriets who provide for our children.

A prestigious group of Fortune 500 business leaders put it this way:

> Many look to the school instead of to parents and community as the frontline defense against every social or health problem from teen pregnancy to child abuse, AIDS, violence, and religious disaffection.
>
> No organization can traverse such a swamp of conflicting missions. Yet, most schools in urban areas and many in suburban and rural communities are pursuing, willingly or not, ever-expanding social and ideological agendas. Few schools have the money, trained personnel, time, or capacity to respond to the increasingly complex social-support needs for their students.
>
> And what is the result of these growing social mandates? School after school is accomplishing neither its academic nor its social goals.[2]

The questions that should be debated more vigorously are these: How widespread should the public schools' responsibility be for fixing social problems? Where is the line between the school's responsibility and the family's? Do schools ultimately hurt families and society when they take responsibility that traditionally has rested with the family? This book examines these questions.

Driving Parents from Schools

Public-education employees complain about lack of parental involve-ment and support. However, it is interesting to note that parents across the board do not avoid involvement in their children's schooling; it's primarily public school parents who do. Less than 15 percent of parents of eighth-graders volunteer at their public school while 50 percent of parents in private schools do. Only 33 percent of public school parents of eighth-graders are active in their PTA while 60 percent of private school parents are.[3] Could this disparity be due, at least in part, to the private schools' limited scope of responsibility that requires parents to take on more responsibility for their children's success?

It is an irony many educators find mystifying: While schools take on more and more responsibilities for the "whole child," parents do not become more involved to help the teachers. In fact, poor relations be-tween parents and teachers have prompted many educators to leave the profession. One survey found that 40 percent of the teachers polled listed lack of parental support and cooperation as their primary reason for considering quitting their careers in education.[4] Yet, in all the fret-ting about lack of parental involvement few people are considering a connection between public employees' moves to expand their roles in raising children and parents' complacency about letting them. This may largely be due to inattentiveness more than protest. While many par-ents like the new responsibilities schools are taking for their children, these parents have found other things to do with their time. While school officials speak more and more about the need for parental involvement, the missions of these schools actually requires less of it.

A key principle in *learning* to be responsible is that people learn to be more responsible as they are called upon to be responsible.[5] This is a basic principle we understand about the development of children, and it doesn't change in adulthood.

Politicians, interest groups, the media, and many parents press schools to do more to solve the problems of our society. However, there are edu-cators who raise the simple point raised by Mary Nebgen, superintendent of the Washoe County school system in Reno, Nevada. After sustaining long-term criticism from the local media regarding educational inequities between rich and poor families, Nebgen made the point we often don't want to hear: "I am being asked to correct the economic state in which some of our students live. I can't do that. I can't fix all that. I can't provide long-term family counseling."[6] But politicians and the education establishment don't believe this. They act as though they haven't seen a social problem that a new program within the schools wouldn't fix.

The crisis that is occurring in public education is due, in large part, to the notion that public schools can and should solve society's faults. Over the last two hundred years American education has undergone a basic shift in educational purposes. Education has always served, to some degree, the larger goals of society. What has changed is the degree to which educators and government leaders rely on education to tackle social, economic, and political problems. In times past, institutions other than schools—churches, charities, legislatures, and businesses—took on the task of addressing these problems. Beginning gradually in the mid-1800s and accelerating in the mid-1900s, public education became the tool for government, attempting to impact problems by addressing them within the schooling years. Rather than give students the basic academic skills in school and allowing them to engage in rigorous discussion regarding social, economic, and political issues as adults, we have, instead, attempted to shape society, the economy, and politics by molding children. In other words, education long ago became a conscious extension of public policy, and its role as public-policy implementer has only increased. Joel Spring, professor of education at the University of Cincinnati, observed:

> As the American school expanded, it penetrated more and more aspects of life. The school became interested in the whole child and the child's family, and these concerns resulted in school involvement in the child's and the family's personal life, health problems, and social life. If the social role of the school continues to expand at the same rate as it did during the previous two centuries, one can predict that by the end of the twenty-first century, the school will be responsible for engineering the total personality and social life

of all citizens and controlling entrance into the labor market. This future role would include responsibility for an individual's work, play, love life, physical and mental health, and political life.[7]

Could it be that Spring's forecast of what school will look like in a hundred years is happening now? While leaders of every stripe cry that our schools are woefully behind the times in technology, in efficiency, and in meeting the needs of our rapidly changing world, could it be that, in at least feeling responsible for the whole child, schools are ahead of the times?

Before examining the problem of public schools' taking more and more parenting responsibilities for raising children we need to understand how public-education leaders attack the traditional family while promoting a new "pro-family" agenda.

2
The New "Pro-Family" Movement

THE POLITICAL LEFT HAS AWAKENED to the pro-family sentiments of Americans and has organized its own "pro-family" parade that it can lead. It is important to note that this renewed interest in the family is not as much about *the family* as it is about *families*. It would be hard to find leaders who are against all family configurations and are truly anti-family in the sense that they are against adults being in long-term relationships with children and committed to their care. However, the new pro-family movement sees no real need to defend and preserve the traditional family.

Probably the biggest and most subtle shift in discussions about the family came in the last two decades. During that time educators and policymakers began to refer to *families* instead of *the family*. They became more sensitive to the diversity of family configurations.

There are many types of families: intact families where both biological parents rear the children, single-parent families, stepfamilies, adoptive families, and co-habitating families in which the parents are not married. Some people have even widened the definition to also include homosexual families in which same-sex partners rear the children.

What we miss in all this discussion of variety is what we really mean by *the family*. The term is as much about describing a norm, a standard, an ideal, as it is a physical description. Policymakers often point out that the traditional family is dying. That may be a definitional problem as much as a reality if the traditional family is defined as a biological mother who is not in the work force at all, and who, along with a biological father, raises only two children. This, of course, doesn't include families in which the mother works from the home or who works part-time but arranges her schedule to be home when the children are home. It doesn't include families with more or fewer than two children. It doesn't include stepfamilies or adoptive families in which the mother stays home to care for the children. And it misses the fact that most people in the many variations of families try their best to simulate the traditional family.

The family is a model. The term is not merely descriptive; it carries moral weight. It consists of a married couple who give birth to and raise children in a nurturing, protective environment. It creates a social framework from which many values hang. If the family is good, then divorce is not good, single-parenting is not good, stepfamilies are not good, and adoptive families (or more precisely abandoned children) are not good. This is not to say that single parents are bad, stepparents are bad, and adoptive parents are bad. It is to say that those family configurations represent "broken families," deviations from the model. It is the morality of such a statement that irks many people.

To make people feel better, the trend is to define a family as just about any configuration of people living together who care for one another. We've solved the problem of broken families by declaring that no family is broken, just different. In their book, *The War Over the Family*, sociologists Peter and Brigitte Berger comment that changing from talking about "the American family" to talking about "American families" altered our standards:

> It is important to note that the empirical fact of diversity is here quietly translated into a norm of diversity. In other words, norms and values, as well as the wishes and hopes of many people are simply bypassed by this definition. Put simply, demography [is] translated into a new morality.[1]

This definition has come with our new sensitivity. But it has come with a price. If, as a society, we broadcast that the family is no longer ideal and that any arrangement is as good as another, it follows that we will get an increase in alternative family arrangements. If the intact family is not special, it is not worth struggling to maintain. Even the newly arranged families struggle because the pattern they seek to emulate—the intact family—is not given a cherished position in society.

Dancing on the Family's Grave

Liberals in the new pro-family movement seem almost happy that the traditional family is staggering under society's pressures. For instance, note the new pro-family stance of Keith Geiger, president of the National Education Association:

> America's families are under siege. And we must come to their aid. For if we, America's educators, are to be effective advocates for children, we must first be effective advocates for parents. We must march to the forefront of the pro-family movement. We must reclaim this territory from all those whose restrictive definition of the term family is derived from watching reruns of "Ozzie and Harriet" and "Leave It to Beaver."[2]

One mother who attended a parent-school meeting to hear about a new "family-friendly" program being implemented at her children's school by Yale University got a shock. "Their opening remarks were, 'Ozzie and Harriet are dead,'" recalled the mother. "And they said our local school provides the answer: full-service day care for children six months and up, from 6 A.M. to 6 P.M., including breakfast. They were telling us, 'Go get a life. We'll raise your kids.'"[3]

It seems liberal leaders can hardly contain their glee that families are moving away from idyllic models of the family. The twist in the new pro-family movement is that rather than focusing on ways to bring the importance of the intact family back to center stage and find ways to make the family self-sustaining and self-caring, it too often seeks to expand government services to unburden parents from their responsibilities. This reflects the view that families are defined by function (any group of people who care for one another) and it matters little who does the function of child-rearing (social worker, day-care worker, teacher) as long as it gets done.

The new pro-family movement sees the value of good parents and stable families but also sees an army of government employees intervening to produce such families. Thus, we find professional caretakers promoting the expansion of professional caretaking—like this coming from Teachers College Press:

> Teachers and administrators, because of their day-to-day contact with students, may have the greatest potential to transmit information, reward efforts and accomplishments, serve as role models, and enhance positive relationships among children. Their effectiveness is enhanced by counselors, psychologists, health professionals, social workers, and sociologists, who are equally involved in schools.[4]

Prominent sociologist James Coleman writes convincingly of how the functions of families—and thus their reasons for existing—have changed over the years. In the nineteenth century and before, children were used for boosting the family income and for caring for their parents in old age. As fathers began to work away from the home, children were no longer contributors to the family business. Still, parents saw their children as investments for increasing family status and for providing for parents in their old age.

Having their children do better than themselves became an important vision for parents. However, as women entered the work force, divorce increased and intact families eroded; children became a burden to parents. As James S. Coleman writes, the family "is an institution relevant to consumption that is no longer important to production." In other words, children cost a lot but contribute little. He further observes that the family's "functional role has been reduced to that of child rearing."[5]

From an economic standpoint, then, children have become a burden to parents rather than an investment. With this in mind, the new pro-family movement considers it helpful to the family to relieve parents of their burdens by having government institutions and programs replace parents in caring for their children.

With the decrease in family and community bonds (what Coleman calls social capital) comes the need for some kind of surrogate. He suggests that the school may be the institution for providing these needs:

> The general shape of the demand for a new institution is clear: It is a demand not for further classroom activities, not for further classroom indoctrination, nor for any particular content, but a demand for child care. It is a demand for care, first, all day from birth to school age; second, after school every day until parents return from work; and, third, all summer.[6]

At least Newt Gingrich only suggested orphanages for parents who are completely unfit. The new pro-family crowd seem to think they should be for everyone. Their vision is of full-service schools allowing children evening and weekend field trips home. If this vision is implemented, they will literally be helping the family to death!

In Defense of the Ideal

Poor Ozzie and Harriet Nelson and Ward and June Cleaver. What did they ever do to deserve such sneering derision? It has become fashionable for liberal leaders to talk of Ozzie-and-Harriet families as archaic notions. But there are clearly problems with this condescending contempt. First, the majority of families are still intact—just like the Nelsons and the Cleavers. Despite the stress the intact family experiences, a majority of children (57.7 percent) live with both biological parents.[7]

Second, while Harriet and June didn't work outside the home, neither do many mothers today, and working women are less loyal to the work force than to their maternal commitments. Working women are eleven times more likely to leave the labor force voluntarily after age twenty-five than are men.[9] Many women who do enter the labor force arrange their schedules so they can still care for their children in an attempt to resemble the Nelsons and the Cleavers.

Third, even though many families today do not look like the television families of the 1950s, surveys indicate that they still hold the Nelsons and the Cleavers as generalized models of what a family should be. For instance, most divorced parents remarry and seek to recreate the two-parent family. A survey of Americans' beliefs about the importance of the family found that 83 percent of Americans agree that "it is better for a child to be born into a two-parent family than to a single mother." Seventy-two percent of those polled said they consider the changes in families over the last thirty years to "have generally been for the worse." Eighty-nine percent of dual-income married couples believe that "young children fare better when they are primarily cared for by their own mother rather than by a day care provider."[10] Maybe the best tribute to the enduring appeal of the model family is that while there are many deviations from the ideal, these deviations strive to simulate the model intact family. In 1990, 72 percent of children lived in two-parent homes.[8]

Finally, research indicates that families that deviate too far from the model set by the Nelsons and the Cleavers tend to have more problems than those that don't. For instance, two researchers point out:

> Preschoolers with a day care center background were found to be more verbally and physically aggressive toward peers and were rated by kindergarten teachers as more hostile than children reared at home. Young children with substantial day care experience may be more peer- than adult-oriented, which at times can cause difficulty in their responses to the teacher's authority upon entrance into formal schooling."[11]

Educational psychology associate professor Cindy I. Carlson writes about the impact of single-parent families:

> Boys in mother-headed single-parent homes, when compared to boys from father-present homes, have higher rates of impulsivity, inattention, antisocial behavior, school discipline problems, and inability to delay gratification.[12]

James Bray and Sandra Berger of the department of family medicine at Baylor College of Medicine report that:

> Compared to their counterparts from nuclear families, children with a stepmother were found to have more conduct

problems in school; and children with a stepfather were found to have more conduct problems and socialized delinquency problems in school. . . . [C]hildren in stepfamilies are also at greater risk of dropping out of high school.[13]

George Gilder, in his book *Wealth and Poverty*, comments on the importance of family on the economic well-being of its members: "[A]fter work the second principle of upward mobility is the maintenance of monogamous marriage and family. . . . [I]t is manifest that the maintenance of families is the key factor in reducing poverty."[14]

In 1987, for instance, 34 percent of women-headed families lived in poverty compared with 25 percent of two-parent families.[15]

Sociologists Peter and Brigitte Berger believe so strongly, not only in the economic importance of the family but also in the socializing and stabilizing importance of the intact family (what they call the bourgeois family), that they passionately write:

> [W]e believe that there is no viable alternative to the bourgeois family for the raising of children who will have a good chance of becoming responsible and autonomous individuals, nor do we see alternative arrangements by which adults, from youth to old age, will be given a stable context for the affirmation of themselves and their values. The defense of the bourgeois family, therefore, is not an exercise in romantic nostalgia. It is something to be undertaken in defense of human happiness and human dignity in a difficult time.[16]

Berger and Berger point out that humans do not have instincts as finely tuned for survival as do animals. For survival humans have institutions to provide guidance in this world. Without institutions each generation would have to reinvent everything. There would be nothing to pass along to succeeding generations because there would be no institutions to do it. The family is the smallest social unit for the procreation and cultivation of each generation. It is the institution for guiding and grooming each wave of humans. Schools cannot provide this same generational grooming because the relationships within the schools are concocted, arbitrary, and transient.

Certainly there are many dysfunctional families in which children and spouses are abused, education and nutrition are neglected, and in which love and stability are hard to find. Still, the family as a norm and an ideal must be held up as the best social institution for raising children and for caring for the elderly. This view may be held by a majority of people, but federal, state, and local education policies often do not support the people who try to maintain this ideal.

Schools are attempting to become the new American family with an army of public employees acting as the children's new mothers, fathers, aunts, and uncles. But this new family is itself dysfunctional, as we shall see.

3
The School As Family

SCHOOLS ARE ATTEMPTING TO BECOME the new family for children. But schools are a dysfunctional family. Part of their dysfunction occurs because many of those involved (from politicians to educators) suffer from what could best be described as codependence, a relationship in which one person feels an overwhelming need to take over those responsibilities that should properly be in the hands of someone else.

The term is most widely used to describe family members surrounding an alcoholic. Each member of the family, especially the spouse, begins to excuse the alcoholic's behavior and tries to fix the messes he or she makes. Codependents find themselves responding to the irresponsible behavior of the alcoholic by either trying to solve all the problems he or she causes or by being stern controllers of the addict. Either way, the codependent takes on more responsibility to make up for the alcoholic's lack of responsibility and enables that person to continue in his or her problem.

This describes the ever-expanding programs in public education. To be sure, many parents act like the irresponsible alcoholic described above. Teachers have a legitimate complaint about the irresponsibility of these parents—their lack of interest and involvement, the lack of support for the student in the home, the lack of communication back to the teacher on the child's progress. Not only are teachers justified in these complaints, they are justified in pointing out the difficulty they have in educating students who come from broken homes, abusive situations, and other family dysfunctions. Teachers are stuck with the mandate of teaching any child who shows up on their doorstep no matter what emotional, mental, and physical condition he or she arrives in.

The Ever-Expanding Mission of the School

Teachers have traditionally felt some responsibility to children and families who need help. Whether it is an after-school chat with a student or even a visit to the home, as long as schools have existed there has been a connection between the school and the home in rearing children. What has changed is the extent to which political and educational leaders wish to institutionalize and expand the school's responsibility in helping families rear their children.

The vision of the education establishment exhibits a kind of educational codependence—that schools are responsible for much more than academic content and skills development. For instance, the Kansas State Department of Education's mission for education has recently changed to read:

> The mission of Kansas education is to prepare each person with the living, learning, and working skills and values necessary for caring, productive, and fulfilling participation in our evolving, global society.[1]

This sounds more like the mission of a family than it does a school. Kansas schools have taken on the responsibility of preparing people with "living" skills, with "values necessary for caring, productive, and fulfilling participation" in society. How are teachers in Kansas to measure a necessary value for caring? What will they deem to be a caring or uncaring attitude? What does "fulfilling participation" look like?

It is the role of parents and family members to raise children with living skills and values. Parents pass on to their children what it means to be a caring and fulfilled individual. These values and skills are shaped by each family's history, culture, religion, and ongoing "conversation" about the purpose and pursuits of "the good life." However, as many— but not most—families prove to be incapable or unwilling to pass on a healthy heritage to their children, schools are beginning to step in to provide this important role for all children.

Of course, teachers have always helped children grow to appreciate the world. The very process of education is the process of imposing meaning on information. There are those conservatives who complain that schools should get away from teaching values and stick with objective knowledge. This misses the point that transferring raw information from the teacher to the student is not education. Such an "objective" transfer of information would turn teachers into computers.

For instance, while it is an objective fact that the Declaration of Independence was signed in 1776, knowing that simple fact hardly constitutes an education. To be educated on the signing of the Declaration of Independence is to know what the creation of that document meant in the formation of the United States or how it changed the relationship between citizens and their government. This is the stuff of meaning-making, not merely information transference. Even in relatively "objective" subjects such as mathematics the imposition of subjective meaning is everywhere. The high esteem we attach to the subject of mathematics reflects our value-orientation to science and technology. The orderliness of mind, logical thinking, and linear progression from the whole to its parts (or vice versa) emphasized in math classes are subtly yet powerfully teaching values regarding the thinking process. Teachers have always conveyed values. If they didn't they wouldn't be teachers.

However, Kansas political and educational leaders now feel it is necessary for public employees in state-run institutions to be responsible for developing people who will have the proper values of caring and self-fulfillment. This is necessary, they believe, because parents are no longer capable or willing to do it.

Yet, even after all this expanded effort by schools to help families, the general public does not seem to appreciate public education any more than it has in the past, and in fact, it continues to criticize public education for doing what people in general perceive to be a poor job. This leaves many teachers bitter and cynical about parents, students, and public education leaders.

The Frustration of Educational Codependence

Teachers express the frustration of educational codependence in much the same language as the wives of alcoholics. For instance, the words of this wife of an alcoholic could be the words of a schoolteacher: "All of a sudden, over the past few years, everything was being put to me. . . . More and more I was taking over the responsibilities for everything."[2]

The codependent often tries to accommodate the irresponsible person's behavior while complaining that it isn't fair. Likewise, school personnel often complain about the irresponsibility of parents while at the same time accommodating the inappropriate behavior. Compare, for instance, the way two wives of alcoholics describe their attempts at accommodating their husbands' lack of commitment to family meals and the way an educational "expert" describes the goals of school breakfast programs as reported in *Education Week*:

- "He'd say he'd be home for dinner . . . [but] he wasn't home by midnight. . . . [I used to] stay awake, trying to be up when he arrived."

- "Sometimes we don't eat until 10 P.M. I'd like to have my daughter in bed and she sometimes does not get to bed until 12 at night."[3]

- "'The days of 'Ozzie and Harriet' are over,' said Ms. Tingling-Clemmons, adding that many families do not have time to provide a nutritious breakfast for their children at home. 'It is our goal to make sure that a morning meal is available to them,' she said."[4]

While school breakfast programs used to be only for the poor, apparently, the parents' lack of time, not just money, to provide breakfast now constitutes a new responsibility for schools. This woman's inflated sense of obligation on this issue is not unique. In 1992, 47,627 schools served 4.16 million children in school breakfast programs. And the trend is for expansion of these programs even to include families who are not economically disadvantaged. Since 1989 breakfast programs have been ex-panded by 6,000 schools. Still, "child advocates" want more to be done to reach more schoolchildren with government-prepared breakfasts.[5]

The question is not whether students and families have many unmet needs; it is whether the school should provide for them. Often, teachers who must teach students who are negatively impacted by social prob-lems welcome the addition of new social services simply because they hope such programs will give them some relief. It is natural and desir-able that teachers are most concerned about the smooth progress of their classes. If certain children disrupt that progression because they have health problems, family distractions, or an empty stomach that makes it hard to pay attention, teachers find it easy to support solutions that offer immediate remedies. An empty stomach can be filled with a school breakfast. A health condition that jeopardizes student attendance can be cured with an on-campus clinic. Students' emotional problems can be addressed more quickly through on-campus counseling services.

The temptation is strong to accept more responsibilities for solving family and social problems. Caught between the mandates of compul-sory education open to the public and parental irresponsibility, teachers see little they can do but attempt to solve the problems themselves. The alternative of admonishing parents to be more responsible seems hope-less. However, being an "enabler" to an irresponsible person seldom reaps the desired outcome. Think of a classroom teacher or a school administrator talking about parents as you read the words of one wife's description of her descent into codependence:

> I know I did support his drinking habit by waiting on him hand and foot. At first I enjoyed it; then I started realizing, well, he doesn't appreciate this, but I kept on. I felt it was my duty. But now I'm learning that I was just one of his supporters. . . . Codependency—it's not obvious right away. It seems like a sharing problem, and it begins to entrap you in a subtle way. I can't say when it was that I began . . . taking over. I never saw it that way. I just saw him busy and stressed and me helping out. Some of my anger was, 'Hey, wait a minute . . . I said that I would help you; all of a sudden I've got the whole ball—take your half.[6]

The Cost of Educational Codependence

There are negative consequences of public schools' compassion in taking on responsibilities traditionally held by families. In what may seem like some kind of cruel law of nature, the very things schools try to eliminate, they may actually enlarge.

Professor Michael Bauman of Hillsdale College points out that we can easily become what he calls the "dangerous Samaritan." He observes that what you pay for is too often exactly what you get—although what you purchased wasn't what you intended.[7] He uses the insurance-company term "moral hazard" to describe this phenomenon. Insurance companies try to avoid providing coverage that will encourage the very disaster they are insuring. If a businessman's sinking company earns less than his fire insurance coverage, his store may soon "mysteriously" catch on fire. If a family's health insurance has no deductible or copayments, the family may visit the doctor more than is really necessary. If auto-insurance coverage is greater than the value of the car, it is worth more in an accident than in the driveway. Bauman makes the point that in these circumstances fire insurance leads to fires, health insurance leads to more "illnesses," and auto insurance leads to accidents. This model of moral hazard can be applied to schools as well.

For example, if schools are encouraged by state governments to provide childcare for families—in essence, rewarding them for not caring for their children—it will be no surprise that those parents will become even less responsible for their children. What is more, by providing free childcare the schools will be encouraging stay-at-home mothers to place their children in the programs and find other things to do with their time. Schools that add after-school childcare will be encouraging mothers who work part-time during school hours (but who are home when their children get home) to increase their work schedules by freeing them from responsibility for their children. Moms who are busy working have less time for involvement at school. In the end, rather than create greater parental participation in education, the schools will reward parents for doing less.

While more schools add breakfast to the list of services to help parents, they are encouraging parents to take less responsibility for their children's nutritional health. In fact, the schools will be penalizing those families that buy their own food for breakfast at home instead of taking advantage of the breakfast program at school. Once breakfast becomes as common as lunch programs in schools it won't be long before legislators will want to offer dinner programs, too. The justification, using the current logic, won't be difficult to make: Two-income families put an undue burden on families to spend time preparing dinner rather than spending quality time in learning-enhancing activities; Mom and Dad can swing by school to pick up their children who are in after-school care and dine at the school cafeteria staffed by high school students learning food-preparation skills for the service industries of the twenty-first century.

In many schools the future is now. Hundreds of public elementary schools have already been transformed from mere schools to what are called "community centers." In these new schools the morning begins with breakfast in the cafeteria and parents dropping off their children in on-site Head Start programs on their way to work. The official school day ends at 3:30 P.M., but pupils stay for an afternoon of activities, snacks, and study time. After work, parents come to the school to pick up their children or to take an evening class on parenting skills. Parents, of course, needn't worry about their children under the school's care because each school has medical and dental facilities as well as a counseling center.[8]

One mother who has her children enrolled in just such a school praises it when she exclaims, "You don't have to fight to get kids to go to this school. It sounds crazy, but the hard part is getting them to leave at the end of the day."[9] It *is* crazy to create government institutions that children prefer over their homes.

The schools are in danger of moving—some would argue they have already moved—from being the extension of a welfare state to a "client state." Rutgers University sociologist David Poponoe defines this as a nation "in which citizens are for the most part clients of a larger group of public employees who take care of them throughout their lives."[10] Is this what we want?

We are swiftly moving away from the idea that schools are primarily about providing academic knowledge and skills to the notion that schools are to provide preventative approaches to social problems. This view unwittingly sees children as both the hope for the future and the prime burden of society. It is the ill-prepared child who will cause America to lose the economic war to other nations. It is the child at home who keeps mothers from pursuing a career. It is the child living in a dysfunctional family who will grow up to create another dysfunctional family, another unproductive worker, or another welfare burden to society. So we think schools can prevent all this from happening. But to do so means that schools provide children with good nutrition, psychological wholeness, preventative healthcare, better socialization, and other child-rearing necessities.

The problem for educators is that families that provide for their own children will be penalized because they will not take advantage of the state-provided programs.[11] The result is that schools then attract the people they complain about the most—parents who aren't responsible. Then the crisis of little parental responsibility for their children's education will be accelerated by the very things designed to supposedly help families. The alcoholic seldom appreciates the efforts of the codependent, and the misguided efforts of the codependent seldom truly help the alcoholic in the long run.

The Consequence of Educational Codependence

Often the things educators implement to solve a problem actually increase the problem or create a new, and sometimes more difficult, one. It's as if Newton's law of action and reaction applies to government. Government's attempts to solve a problem by hitting it with a new program cannot happen in isolation. The collision of problem A and intended remedy B happens in a social universe that is packed with other things. The problem may be removed, but it is now replaced with new factors created by the remedy. Often these factors cause problems that are greater, or at least equal to, the original problem. A small problem becomes a big one. A minor social headache becomes a migraine. A crisis accelerates. You can find this acceleration in many areas of education.

- Massachusetts implemented a bilingual education law in an attempt to help non–English-speaking students. The Transitional Bilingual Education Law dictated that when there are twenty or more students in a school who share the same language they must be provided a bilingual education in all courses (rather than an intensive English course to help them succeed in regular classes). This was intended to be a remedy to the problem of low achievement among these students. However, many students naturally felt comfortable in the classes that taught them in their native language, and they chose to stay there. When their time in the program ended after five or six years, the students found themselves in the same predicament of being unable to assimilate into regular courses. The result: They dropped out of school.[12]

- Busing students across town to gain racial balance in schools has gone by the wayside in many school districts—a result of crisis acceleration. For example, in 1972 Oklahoma City schools introduced mandatory busing to bring racial balance to its schools that were predominately minority populated. In 1984 mandatory busing was halted due to its failure to integrate the schools. Rather than solve the problem, busing increased it.

  James Coleman, the man whose 1966 report on racial inequity spurred the move to mandatory busing, issued a report as early as 1975 noting that busing brought about greater segregation due to "white flight" and the resulting concentrations of blacks in certain schools.[13]

- Sex education has always been a controversial issue in public schools. Schools cannot be blamed for the exploitation of sex in movies, on television, in magazines, and in teen fashion that has also caused the degradation of youth. "Aiding and abetting" our culture's attack on youth's sexuality may be a better description of sex education courses. Whether it is seen as the cause or as a co-conspirator in the problem, it is evident that sex education has had a part in the crisis acceleration in sexual behavior. During the 1980s, for instance, the Center for Disease Control reported that condom use rose dramatically from 28 percent to 45 percent among sexually active white teenage girls. (Black teens' use remained around 30 percent.) Yet pregnancy rates did not go down. The reason for this, according to the CDC, was because more girls were engaging in sexual activity.[14]

Susan Tew of the Alan Guttmacher Institute, which contributed to the CDC's report, commented, "We don't know how effective condom use has been when you look at the fact that the pregnancy rate hasn't dropped and more teenagers are using birth control."[15] Part of the answer lies in the fact, as the CDC reported, that condom failure rate for teenagers was 26 percent—the highest among any age group it studied. The cost of the intended remedy for teen pregnancy—explicit sex education—comes at the price of increased teen sexual callousness and aggressiveness.

- Courses designed to teach values use "value-neutral" nonjudgmental techniques that have led to students with little or no conscience about their antisocial behavior. Schools respond to this new crisis with "conflict resolution" courses that help students develop "communication skills" but don't help them form moral consciences.

- Gang violence led at least one school district to pilot a program that led third-grade students in hypnotic visualization exercises to create peaceful attitudes. The program purported to help children find, set, and achieve goals in their lives. It did this by introducing them to necromancy—contacting the dead. With this program, schools accelerated right out of education and into mysticism:

  > How would you like a special or custom-built house [in your mind] to go to anytime you want to, with anything you want in it? You could have any person you want to come and visit you. It wouldn't matter if he or she was dead or alive, real or imaginary. After today, you will always have this special place and special way of being with anyone you want.[16]

- Educators' worries over low self-esteem among students have led them to implement gimmickry that does nothing to lift self-esteem while it takes away from precious time spent on the one thing proven to increase self-esteem in school—academic achievement. In fact, the idea that "learning should be fun" as a means to greater achievement and higher self-esteem has been shown to undermine a strong work ethic in young people.[17]

- The government's Supplemental Security Income program, designed to help families with severely disabled children, was expanded in 1990 to include children with learning disabilities. Students are now encouraged, with the incentive of government paychecks, to disrupt classrooms and fail in school. Educators tell stories of students who are coached by their parents to pretend to be learning impaired in order to receive money. When one teacher asked a nine-year-old student why he was so disruptive, he responded: "If I get better, my mother will beat me, because we need the crazy money."[18]

Public education's mission has changed. William Davis, professor of education at the University of Maine, reflects the new thinking about the role of education:

To assume that education is exclusively about cognition and learning and that teaching is exclusively about imparting academic skills represents a narrow view of both learning and teaching. . . . Today's and tomorrow's schools must have a broader vision and mission. Like it or not, today's and tomorrow's teachers are (or will be) in a very real (if not credentialed) sense social workers, mental-health workers, and health workers.[19]

Unfortunately, education policymakers concentrate on how effectively they can assume the responsibilities rather than what they can do to assist greater parental and community responsibility.

What is needed to revitalize the family and reinvigorate public education is counter-intuitive. Instead of being pro-family by expanding government assistance programs that result in making family duties irrelevant, schools need to narrow their missions. Our faith in people's ability and ingenuity to solve their problems through their personal, familial, religious, and community resources must be stronger. These bonds tend to exert moral pressure on responsible behavior that is largely absent from government programs. But with the exception of a few experiments in charter schools, vouchers, and other such liberating programs, education leaders want government, through schools, to take on more family responsibilities. We'll look at some of those responsibilities in the next chapter.

4
Caring for the Whole Child

G EORGE ORWELL ENVISIONED a future in which government became Big Brother, watching and controlling all aspects of life. Our future could more accurately see government acting as Big Nanny, "nurturing" all aspects of our lives.

You can see the Big Nanny syndrome in the current talk about preschool programs. Policymakers hold up successful preschool programs as models for childcare provided by public schools. A growing number of people call for preschool programs beginning at infancy. The Abecedarian Project in Chapel Hill, North Carolina, for instance, reports success among high school teens who participated in its program as infants. The study involved children in an all-day childcare center all year long at the University of North Carolina. The *average* age of children entering the program was four and a half months. There was one caregiver for every three infants. By the time the children were four years old, the ratio was one caregiver for every four children. The cost of this program in 1986 dollars was eight thousand dollars per year for each child. By the time each child entered kindergarten the government had spent almost forty thousand dollars per child.[1]

What the program really proves is that good parenting and full-time attention to a child from infancy can have a positive impact on a child's education. Isn't this obvious? Rather than pay public employees eight thousand dollars per year per child in a program that would draw children away from parents, imagine what would happen if the government gave mothers an eight-thousand-dollar annual tax break per child for staying at home with their children. However, this kind of encouragement to parenting is not about to happen. Instead, policymakers talk about preschool "intervention" to ensure greater success than could be achieved by parents themselves.[2]

Public schools have for many years been the conduit for government policies because they are state-run institutions most children must attend. The most direct way to reach children with a government program is in the government buildings they attend every day. As state and federal governments feel the need to correct people's problems, the schools become the natural hypodermic for injecting the government's medicine.

A Seventy-Billion-Dollar Hypodermic

In 1965 Congress created a program called Chapter 1 as an effort to help schools meet the special needs of disadvantaged children who live in areas with particularly high concentrations of low-income families. Since then the government has sent more than $70 billion to schools through Chapter 1. By 1992 this funding accounted for 19 percent of the U.S. Department of Education's total budget or $6.1 billion to help five million children or one in nine students in America.[3]

While ways of figuring poverty vary, educational policymakers look to studies such as the UNICEF report that just over 20 percent of children in America are living in poverty, and this is after welfare and food stamp programs have been counted.[4] Another study claims a link between chronic poverty and lower IQ scores in children as well as increased fearfulness, depression, temper tantrums, and aggression.[5] Studies such as these fuel educational leaders' justification for expanding programs to provide more services for children and families.

However, there is another way to interpret the data. Robert Rector, a senior policy analyst with the Heritage Foundation, sees the erosion of "middle-class values" as the main factor contributing to lower IQ and increased behavior problems with poor children. His concern is that federal programs that increase benefits to the poor tend to hurt middle-class values rather than advance them.

For instance, the study's researchers pointed out that behavior problems in poor children were closely linked to the families that were headed for a long time by single mothers who never married or families that suffered divorces that left the mothers to raise the children alone. They admitted, however, that they focused on the issue of poverty rather than family structure because poverty is more open to government tinkering than are interpersonal relationships.[6] This explains, in part, how schools get drawn into expanding their responsibilities.

Now that politicians have decided that schools should not just be about learning, educators have added an array of other social services to their responsibilities. Let's look at a few of these new areas.

Mental Health

The mental health of schoolchildren is an emerging concern of policymakers alarmed by reports such as that from the National Health/ Education Consortium, a coalition of fifty-seven national health and education organizations. They report that "between 12 percent and 15 percent of children in the United States suffer mental disorders, including attention-deficit disorder, hyperactivity, conduct disorder, depression, and alcohol and other drug abuse." Their solution? Have schools put more mental-health professionals (like themselves) on the payroll as well as increase funding for treatment and prevention programs.[7] "'Let the teachers teach,' we say. But first, children have to be ready to learn," writes Dr. James Tompkins in his book on applying therapeutic models to teaching techniques. "Children and teachers cannot be expected to succeed in schools unless they receive the support necessary to break down those barriers to learning that exist in families, communities, and schools. We must refurbish an innovative track to healing and successful achievement."[8]

Educators see the emotional scars students carry with them to school. Every teacher, for instance, knows how the divorce of a student's parents can negatively impact his or her performance in school. Add to this common stress other conditions such as parental substance abuse, the child's loneliness due to both parents' working, and the repercussions from poor parenting skills, and the classroom becomes a complex mixture of emotions—some exploding, some imploding.

In response to this, children's self-help groups are a growing phenomenon in schools with children as young as five years old. Groups of children began forming in the early 1980s with the encouragement of teachers and counselors to talk about family problems and support one another.[9] Feeling the need to solve the emotional problems of students, schools rush in with sponsored programs like "It's Up to Me," in Texas. It contains exercises that have children complete sentences such as: "If I had twenty-four hours to live . . . ," "If I had a gun I would . . . ," "People can hurt my feelings most by . . . ," "I am hurt most easily when . . . ," "I am afraid to . . . ," "I feel most mistreated when . . . " The children in this program are required to select from a list of thirty-six ways to respond to stress. The list includes: smoke, hate myself, think about suicide, take drugs, shoplift, lie about things, drink, skip school, vandalize, stay away from my family, feel like running away, and steal.[10] After the Los Angeles riots that were sparked by the verdict in the trial of police officers accused of beating Rodney King, Los Angeles school officials sent an army of counselors into the schools to help the 640,000 students "deal with all the related issues and responses."[11] School officials, it seems, felt that parents themselves couldn't adequately discuss the feelings their children might have had.

Healthcare

There is a steady push by many child-health-policy lobbyists to put clinics on school campuses or to have a link between schools and nearby off-campus clinics. Almost five hundred on-campus clinics are now in operation nationwide.[12] A study done by the Employee Benefit Research Institute reports that nearly ten million children were uninsured in 1992.[13] One influential commission on helping families in poor neighborhoods advocates that schools "should help out family needs as well as those of children by integrating health and social services into the support system for Chapter 1 families." Recognizing that federal funding alone is not sufficient for this they further call for states to "accept responsibility for preparing a plan to eliminate health and social barriers to learning."[14] There is that phrase again, "accept responsibility." What is not seriously being questioned among decision-makers with influence is this: Even if states had the money to throw at these problems, it is not only wrongheaded to think that these problems will be eliminated, it must be questioned whether government has any "responsibility" to tackle them. Still, politicians and education leaders press on with more burdens for schools.

The National Association of School Boards encourages the expansion of the federal government in actively promoting healthcare in schools. They advocate ideas ranging from $500,000 in grants for schools to develop a comprehensive K-12 health-education curriculum to a national office on school health in the U. S. Health and Human Services Department.[15] This kind of action is justified by leaders because of the reports that criticize the current condition of children's health. The American Health Foundation, for instance, in 1993 issued a report card on the nation's success in handling children's health issues in which the country received a C-grade.[16] It seems that, for some, the existence of the problem is justification enough for relieving parents from the responsibility of guarding the health of their children.

Parents, it seems, generally show considerable support for schools' taking on what was formerly a family responsibility. A 1992 poll found 77 percent of the public favored the idea of using school facilities to deliver health and social services to students. Only 16 percent of those polled opposed the idea.[17] Large majorities of public-school parents want schools to be responsible for examinations to detect sight and hearing defects (94 percent in favor), free or low-cost lunches (93 percent in favor), inoculations against communicable diseases (83 percent in favor), free or low-cost breakfasts (80 percent in favor), and dental examinations (61 percent in favor).[18] Parents also seem to want schools to dispense condoms to students even without a clinic on campus. Sixty-five percent of public-school parents favor condom distribution in schools, although 23 percent of those would at least require parental consent.

The term "one-stop shopping" is now used in education circles to describe the idea that a school should be the central delivery system, or at least the administrative center, for a wide range of health, social, and childcare needs. Experts who train educators as well as administrators advocate this expanded role for schools. The American Association of State Colleges and Universities, an organization whose member institutions train more than half the nation's teachers, predicts the changing role of schools to what it calls "community-service centers." These centers will focus not only on students but their families as well.[19] This is a backdoor way to implement socialized medicine.

The role of school-district superintendents and school principals has changed dramatically as well and will continue to change as the structure and function of schools change. The National Policy Board for Educational Administration points out that with the "one-stop shopping" model of schools, principals take on new responsibilities in leadership and problem solving.[20] Indeed, the principal's new job description will include being a hospital administrator.

In 1993 Minnesota Governor Arne Carlson proposed that all of the state's education and social services be combined into one agency to serve children from the time they are born until they become young adults. His proposal so fused the idea that schools and social services should be linked that his plan called for this new agency to replace the state's education department.[21]

The growing support both by the public and by policymakers for collaboration of health and social agencies and schools means that expanding the responsibility of government employees for the care of children will increase. It is this sense that schools must provide what parents can't or won't that reflects educational codependence. One educational leader expresses this sense of overresponsibility when she writes that schools must house various social-service agencies because "services need to come to people. This means focusing on where people work, where they live, and especially where children go to school."[22] It apparently is not enough to have the services available for people; now they must also be brought to the people who need them.

Childcare

One of the latest nonacademic responsibilities being thrust upon schools is childcare. Local schools are under pressure to respond to the growing need for full-time childcare for working parents. By the year 2000 it is estimated by some that three out of four children will have working mothers.[23] The trend is for more mothers to quickly reenter the work force. Between 1981 and 1991 the percentage of women who went back to work before their babies' first birthday leaped 60 percent to represent more than half of all new mothers.[24] In 1976, 19 percent of births were to women in their thirties. By 1991 this rose to around 33 percent.[25] Since many of these women work, this has dramatically increased the need for daily, long-term childcare. Currently, 5.7 million children aged three to five receive care and education from people other than their parents. This represents over 66 percent of children in that age bracket.[26] Even bigger numbers are touted by the Council of Chief State School Officers. They report that ten million preschool children need childcare while an additional thirteen million school children need after-school care.[27]

This reality, along with the federal government's national education goal that "all children will enter school ready to learn," puts pressure on schools to act. Sixty-seven percent of public-school parents support childcare centers in the public school system for preschool children and 69 percent want after-school care for pupils.[28] Educational leaders claim that 70 percent of current childcare arrangements are inadequate because the caregivers lack training.[29] Thus, they reason that schools must provide the professional care.

The issue of childcare is ripe for thrusting the responsibility for caregiving on local school districts. Yet this new role will come at the cost of increased financial burdens for districts. The Childcare Employee Project studied the problem of high turnover (26 percent greater than all U.S. companies report) and low quality of care in day-care centers. They concluded that low wages and lack of healthcare coverage for employees were major contributors to the problem.

This means that as school districts take on the day-care role they will need to increase wages and provide medical benefits to caregivers. Publicly funded childcare workers will mean an entirely new constituency because teachers unions will be brought into districts and contract negotiations will, over time, result in increasing costs to taxpayers. As one policy adviser put it, "We want to make this a career people are really proud of and able to carry on."[30] To provide such a system of care, some experts estimate the cost will reach twenty-three billion dollars each year.[31] These part-time orphanages will be expensive.

Head Start

Proponents of public-school childcare point to large cost-benefit ratios in preschool programs. The highly touted Perry preschool experiment in Ypsilanti, Michigan, for instance, reported that for every dollar spent in the program $7.16 was saved in other public programs.[32] This study followed into adulthood 123 poor children who had participated in the program at ages three and four. It evaluated such things as their dropout rates, crime rates, earning level, and marriage rates. The study found that in many respects children who graduated from the preschool program were dramatically better off than those who did not. Successes in programs such as Perry's are held up by advocates of government-sponsored preschools as justification for greater school action. This preventative-investment argument is powerful when presented to budget-strapped legislators and tax-weary citizens.

Yet, policymakers need to consider other views. Opponents of Head Start expansion caution that the Perry preschool program is an unusually controlled environment and does not represent the majority of preschool programs.[33] It is very difficult to replicate successful school programs that have the enthusiasm and dedication of the original pilot program.

Howard Richman, a research associate in cognitive psychology at Carnegie-Mellon University, points to the fact that these programs have the effect of temporarily boosting children's IQ scores long enough to help them avoid being labeled handicapped and retained in early grades. One successful Head Start study, for instance, divided children into two groups and measured their IQs. The average IQ of children who were to be enrolled in the program was 89 and the IQ of those not to be in the program was 87. When measured just after participating in the program the children's IQs rose to an average of 96. Yet, by age seventeen the children's IQs had dropped to 89, which was still only 2 points higher than those who did not enroll in Head Start.

However, Richman calls attention to the fact that when the children entered elementary school fewer were labeled handicapped or received grade retention. This, he concludes, was the reason these children did not drop out of school later and why they went on to greater success in life than other children. In other words, the children's success appears to have more to do with how the school responded to them than how well Head Start helped them throughout their entire public education.

Richman also points out that because the program required teachers to make daytime home visits more children enrolled in the program had stay-at-home mothers than those children in the control group.[34]

Advocates of Head Start and similar programs acknowledge the enormous strain the proposed expansion would put on the education system. And the gains they look at are not necessarily measurable. One official involved in the Genesee County, Michigan, Head Start program admits that Head Start's gains are "not always very measurable" but says the program should also be judged by "how many children are able to adjust and have positive self-esteem."[35]

While the pragmatic arguments for government-run social programs abound among policymakers, little justification is offered for why all this nurturing should come from state employees. For example, certainly it alleviates a mother's current problem to have free childcare at the local school, but is it right for the government to provide it? Proponents of the ever-expanding role of government make a direct connection between a need and a government solution and circumvent the responsibility of the individual. Note the personal sense of responsibility expressed by one group of policy advisers advocating the connection between school and childcare: "Until we establish the link between childcare and education—both in policy and in program dimensions—we will continue to shortchange our children and their families."[36] Wrong. We shortchange children and their families by making it easy and painless for parents to dump parenting responsibilities onto someone else. Politicians need to stop seeing parents merely as breeders and workers. They need to adjust current policies so that parents and extended family members have better incentives to return to the task of actually raising their children.

Troubles in the Orphanage

THE MOTHER DESCRIBED her family as "All-American." She and her husband work in the medical profession; they have four children, and she is active in her son's Little League baseball. She and her son watch television together and discuss issues such as violence and gangs when they appear on the TV set.

Still, one day in early October, her thirteen-year-old son packed a .38 caliber revolver, a .22 caliber derringer, an eighteen-inch machete, and a dagger in his book bag and went to school plotting with two other boys to "take over" a classroom full of students at their suburban middle school. Their plan was foiled when another student notified the principal after they showed him the weapons while on the playground.

What would cause such unusual behavior? Maybe it was his listening to the hard rock group Pearl Jam sing about a boy who takes a gun to school. Maybe it was the violent video game Mortal Combat that one of the boys played every morning at a nearby liquor store before school. Maybe it was just another day in violent America—another story in the growing saga of senseless youth violence. Whatever the reason, more and more students inside schools act out in defiance of authority and social norms. If schools try to solve the antisocial problems of young people by becoming surrogate parents they will find themselves in a continual downward spin of despair. Rather than help parents be parents, expanded school services free them from being parents. Their children, then, will continue to come to school with family problems. A vicious cycle ensues: Schools provide more services, parents shift responsibility for their children to the schools, and schools stagger under the weight of more troubled children and add more services.

Let's look at a few of the troubles our public schools encounter.

Youth Violence

Violence among children and teenagers seems to rage out of control. In 1988 murder accounted for just over half of all firearm-related deaths among teenagers ages fifteen to nineteen. Among children between the ages of ten and fourteen, murder accounted for 35 percent of firearm-related deaths; and among children aged one to nine years old more than half of all such deaths were murders.[1] Among white teenagers the murder rate by firearms for teenagers fifteen to nineteen reached 14 people per 100,000 by 1990, more than doubling since 1985. For black youth the figure tripled during the same period, reaching 105.3 people per 100,000.[2] Between 1986 and 1990 gun-related murders took the lives of 65 students and six school personnel.[3] One study reports that 13 percent of gun-related problems occur in elementary and preschools.[4]

A 1990 survey conducted by the Centers for Disease Control found that 20 percent of high school students polled said they carry some kind of weapon to school at least once a month.[5] A 1993 survey conducted by the Harvard School of Public Health reports that 4 percent of students ranging in ages from 10 to 19 claimed they have carried a gun to school in the past year. The picture that emerges indicates a real problem of violence or threats of violence among students.

Of Classrooms and Coffins

The problem is not just with guns. Knives are more readily available and easier to hide. Three boys burst into a social studies class in the suburban town of Dartmouth, Massachusetts, and stabbed a sixteen-year-old schoolmate to death. The assailants wielded a knife, a billy club, and a baseball bat. While the teacher wrestled with the boy carrying with the bat, the other two set upon the victim, Jason Robinson. He died within an hour. The reason for the murder? He was the friend of a boy who had been in a hallway scuffle with the three attackers. When they couldn't find their initial target, they stabbed his friend.[6]

The rate of minors going to jail increased by 41 percent between 1979 and 1988.[7] In suburban communities violent crime such as murder, rape, robbery, and aggravated assault increased 11.8 percent, and in rural areas it increased 17.7 percent from 1990 to 1991.[8] Out of 720 public school districts polled, 590 (82 percent) reported that violence had increased from 1989 to 1994.[9] These kinds of statistics have prompted at least one school district to consider providing burial insurance for its low-income students.[10]

Threatened Teachers

In Columbus, Georgia, three girls and four boys in a sixth-grade class at Georgetown Elementary School were arrested for making two attempts at killing their teacher. When their attempt at poisoning the teacher's iced tea failed they later tried to trip her down a staircase. School officials also found a gun and a knife in their possession. Their reason for trying to murder their teacher? She made them behave in class.[11]

In 1991, 19 percent of public-school teachers nationwide reported being verbally abused by students within the four weeks prior to the survey; 8 percent reported being threatened within the last year.[12] For example, in Lorain, Ohio, two seventh-grade girls were charged with plotting to stab their English teacher to death because she had scolded one of the girls earlier in the day. At least a dozen other students wagered up to two hundred dollars on whether the girls would go through with it. Authorities, tipped off by a student, intercepted the girls just minutes before their scheduled attack. As a school administrator entered the room to stop the girls, others in the class whispered, "Get her now!" A twelve-inch knife was confiscated from the book bag of one of the girls—an honor student.[13]

Over two percent (approximately fifty thousand teachers!) said they were physically attacked within the last year. Interestingly, while teachers in cities reported the highest incidence of verbal abuse (28 percent) and threats (15 percent), the same percentage were physically attacked as teachers in suburban and small town schools—3 percent.[14]

In high-achieving schools, teachers reported feeling safest. Seventy-seven percent of those teachers reported feeling "very safe" while only 44 percent of teachers felt safe in low-achieving schools. Twenty-eight percent of districts reported a problem with students assaulting teachers. *Education Week* reported that the survey of teachers also found that violence tends to disproportionately affect schools with large minority populations.[15]

Ethnic strife and gang activity are often big contributors to school violence. In a study of ninety-four small cities with populations from 50,000 to 150,000, almost one-third reported that gang violence is a "major problem."[16] Fairfax County, Virginia, police recently assigned a police officer full time to Annandale High School, where racial fights have become a part of the school's routine. One year the fights were between rival Hispanic and Korean students. The next year the violence involved black and Hispanic teens. In one day fifty students were sent home for brawling. The next day, fourteen students were arrested because of student violence.[17] And the national rap sheet goes on:

- A fourteen-year-old member of the Simon City Royals gang in Springfield, Illinois, was shot on the stairs of Ridgley Elementary School.

- A school security guard was shot by an eighth-grade gang member after the guard broke up a fight between rival gang members.

- Guns and knives are not necessary for violence on campuses. Sixty black and Puerto Rican students in a Milwaukee high school fought in the school auditorium immediately after a weapons check conducted by school officials.[18]

- The Los Angeles schools have created "safe-passage corridors" using police prominently placed on certain streets to protect students who have to travel through gang territory to get to school each day.[19]

- A five-year-old boy brought a loaded .22-caliber pistol to his elementary school in Monroe, Louisiana. In Calhoun, Louisiana, another boy, nine years old, brought a gun to school. In Oakland, California, school officials confiscated ten guns, fifty-two knives, and eleven replica weapons from their elementary students.[20] In a kind of grave-digger humor, a popular fax being sent among teachers is a mock "high school math proficiency exam." It includes such questions as: "Johnny has an AK47 with a thirty-round clip. If he misses six out of ten shots and shoots thirteen times at each drive-by shooting, how many drive-by shootings can he attempt before he has to reload?"

Violence and the Media

Schools are stuck having to deal with the children that show up at their door. Unfortunately, today's students arrive in class having fed on an enormous diet of electronic violence. Television, video games, movies, and certain types of music provide a constant message: Violence solves problems.

Most children can, it seems, separate reality from fantasy and disassociate themselves from the dramatized violence they see through electronic media. Still, there are tens of thousands of children who are influenced toward violence by the fictional violence they see. It is unconvincing for those in the entertainment industry to argue that violent images do not spawn violent actions in people. These same producers want us to believe that watching one hour of violence will have no effect on the viewer while a thirty-second commercial selling a breakfast cereal will. Of course the violence a child watches has an effect. And on some children the effects are quite literally deadly.

On average, children watch as much television each week as they spend at school. They enter the first grade already having seen thousands of hours of television. In fact, by the time a child enters first grade he or she has cumulatively spent more than one year in front of the tube.[21] In the midst of this the school is expected to maintain discipline and provide a safe environment for students. It's as if we as a society purposely make it as difficult as possible for teachers to do their jobs. In many instances we have turned our schools into a new kind of juvenile detention center that keeps its inmates during business hours and releases them to the custody of their parents at night. But if schools are going to teach students they must maintain discipline and order. They cannot be responsible for solving the problems of troubled youth and families.

While schools struggle to prevent students from hurting each other, they also have had the burden thrust upon them of preventing students from using drugs and alcohol and hurting themselves.

Drugs and Alcohol

After a decade of decline, drug use among teenagers is on the rise. One nationwide survey of approximately fifty thousand students found that 31 percent of high school seniors in 1993 said they had used drugs in the previous twelve months. This was up from 27.1 percent in 1992. The survey also found a 4.1 percent increase of marijuana use among twelfth-graders.[22] The study found that high-schoolers' use of LSD, cigarettes, and other stimulants was also up.

Another survey found slight increases of drug use among eighth-grade students from 1991 to 1992. Pollsters found that eighth-graders surveyed were "significantly less likely" than eighth-graders the year before to consider cocaine and crack cocaine as dangerous.[23] The good news is that 89.6 percent of eighth-graders said they disapprove of people who try cocaine even once.

A third study done during the 1992–1993 school year found that use of hallucinogens among sixth- to eighth-graders increased slightly.[24] Teachers find they sometimes must contend with the presence of drugs even in the elementary grades. Six fourth-graders in a school in Tampa, Florida, for instance, were caught carrying bags of cocaine to school and passing them around class. Obviously, these children got the drugs from an adult, most likely a relative.

Teenage drinking is another problem for schools. Nationwide teenagers drink at an alarming rate. A 1993 report by the National Institute on Drug Abuse states that ten million students from seventh to twelfth grade have consumed alcohol. Eight million drink on a weekly basis, and 500,000 "binge" drink until they are drunk.[25] In 1989, 19 percent of the fifteen- to nineteen-year-olds who died in automobile accidents had alcohol in their blood. By 1993 that figure had risen to 33 percent.[26]

Another study found that one in five high school students admitted to driving a car while intoxicated within the last year and one out of twelve admitted to driving drunk at least four or five times in the past twelve months.[27]

Families Have Let Us Down

Teaching values has always been the mandate for educators. However, today's teachers find themselves working harder to simply maintain a moderate level of decency among many young people.

Has anyone asked why it should be the responsibility of the schools to make a special subject out of character education? I agree we need it, but isn't it strange that the subject has to be so deliberately taught and that schools must lead the way in this? We have grown so accustomed to courses on drug education, alcohol abuse, and decision-making skills that these subjects seem as basic to education as do math and English. But why must schools do this? What ever happened to parents, neighbors, and the community teaching these lessons, and schools merely chiming in with their support?

One answer may lie in the fact that parents simply aren't there for children. One-quarter of eighteen-year-olds live with only one parent. This figure rose from 12 percent in 1960 to 25 percent in 1990.[28] The fastest-growing segment of single parents are those who never married. Stepfamilies account for the fastest-growing type of family structure. Eric Miller of Research Alert, a marketing forecasting firm, predicts that by the year 2000 stepfamilies will be more common than traditionally intact families.[29] Miller predicts that as the family structure changes so will its definition:

> As we approach the end of the century, "being there" is becoming as thick as blood. Those who give care are "family." Child care, eldercare, and just plain taking care in general are becoming progressively more important as a result of the fragmented family structure.[30]

But just "being there" does not have the same effect on children as does the presence of both parents. For instance, in studying what best prevented boys from dropping out of school, researchers found that the presence of both parents at home is a strong influence in keeping boys in school. It effectively counters even the negative influence poverty can play in dropout rates.[31] Another study of Census Bureau research found that 34 percent of recently divorced mother-child families who were previously above the poverty line dropped into poverty after the divorce. Almost 50 percent of black mother-child families suffered the same consequence of divorce.

The research also discovered that two-income families divorced more frequently than did families in which the father worked full time and the mother worked only part time.[32] Thus it seems obvious that keeping families together should be a place to start in the formation of policy. We need to find economic, legal, and social incentives to keep families intact. Parents need greater tax rewards for staying together, marriages should be legally harder to dissolve, and there needs to be a greater social conscience that praises marriage and frowns on divorce. In today's social climate we attach a more negative stigma to smoking or wearing fur than we attach to divorce.

Family mobility is another contributor to behavioral problems and low academic performance among students. New research has found that how frequently a family moves can be as powerful a predictor of student problems as other factors such as poverty, race, lack of parental education, and single-parent-family status. Researchers for the *Journal of the American Medical Association* examined the records of 9,915 students from first through twelfth grade looking for how family mobility affected student performance. They found that students who moved at least six times during their schooling "were 77 percent more likely than those with few or no moves to have four or more behavior problems, and 35 percent more likely to fail a grade."[33]

Another study revealed that 28 percent of fourth-graders moved one or two times within a two-year period and dropped twelve points on math proficiency tests; 13 percent moved three or more times and dropped twenty-five points on math tests. Eighteen percent of eighth-graders moved one or two times during a two-year period and dropped twelve points while 4 percent moved three or more times and dropped twenty-six points.[34]

When both parents work there is also greater stress when they arrive home. Fifteen corporations financed a study of thirty-four hundred workers and found that there were more than three times as many stresses at home over work issues than there were stresses at work over family issues.[35] Just over half of working parents spend less than two hours a week caring for their children and "42 percent spend no time reading to the kids."[36] Even when families eat dinner together they do so without significant interaction. A Gallup poll found that almost four out of ten people who eat dinner together do so while watching television or reading.[37]

What's a School to Do?

In response to the disintegrating family, one district started a program called "Home Alone 3." This special course trained elementary and middle school children in coping with being alone all day after school. In discussion groups students swapped advice for how to deal with it: "Watch TV, go to a friend's house," suggested one boy. Another young teen suggested, "Take a couple of sodas, lie down on the couch, and watch MTV." One thirteen-year-old told the group how she has "made the best of it" by learning to be responsible for caring for her young brother and sister, cleaning the house, cooking meals, and being "in charge."[38] In other words, becoming a thirteen-year-old parent.

However, policymakers move in the wrong direction when they respond to these problems by restructuring schools to allow parents to continue in their child-neglecting behavior. Instead of demanding that parents be responsible, government policymakers unwittingly enable parents to continue in their child-destructive habits. They usually talk in terms of expanding services to support families, yet these services only make it easier for parents to continue leaving the rearing of their children in the hands of someone else. Increasingly this role is falling on the shoulders of educators.

Schools try hard to make up for the deficiencies of parents, but their efforts often have little effect on the lives of children. After years of drug and alcohol education courses in schools Surgeon General Antonia Novello in 1993 considered the nation's efforts to curb underage drinking only "mediocre."[39] A Rand Corporation study found that drug education programs "lose their effectiveness once the lessons have ended." They did a seven-year study of teenagers who went through drug education as seventh- and eighth-graders. By ninth grade, the researchers found, "the positive impact had disappeared." Though the students retained their knowledge of the negative impact of drugs into the tenth grade, the drug education did not significantly alter their behavior.[40]

The U.S. Department of Justice commissioned an independent research group to spend $300,000 and three years to study the effectiveness of a popular antidrug program used in schools called DARE—Drug Abuse Resistance Education. The researchers studied the effects of DARE's specially trained local police officers presenting the program to fifth- and sixth-graders in seventeen weekly forty-five- to sixty-minute sessions. They concluded that DARE was statistically insignificant in preventing drug use among students. Nationwide, schools spend $750 million a year using DARE, so it is not surprising that many educators rejected the findings.[41]

Similar findings related to antismoking programs in schools. After schools have spent years and millions of dollars teaching students the harmful effects of smoking, the University of Michigan's Institute for Social Research reports that the same proportion of high school seniors smoked in 1989 as in 1981—29 percent.[42] In other words, if one goal of antismoking programs is to have fewer young people smoking by the time they graduate, it has utterly failed.

Self-Esteem Programs and Drugs

Schools have tried to deal with student substance abuse by addressing the self-esteem problems arising from family dysfunctions. Drug education programs such as Quest, Project Charlie, Pumsey, and DUSO incorporate a strong emphasis on self-esteem and feelings. The theory is that by dealing with children's emotional problems schools will stem the desire of students to experiment with drugs. However, research has found this does not work well.

A study published in the *Psychology in the Schools* journal reviewed twenty-three affective (feelings-oriented) education programs used in elementary schools and found they had little effect on students' emotional well-being or behavior. William Strein of the University of Maryland's college of education conducted the review of research and concluded that "the lack of positive significant findings in the more carefully designed studies provides little support for the effectiveness of affective education programs in promoting positive changes on either behavioral or affective measures, especially for programs with an internal focus."[43]

He found in his review of various studies that when a "placebo" group of students was used to compare to the students in the affective program there was almost a "complete lack of supportive evidence" that the affective education program was beneficial. Strein concluded that "the evidence for changing self-concept, or other internal/affective outcome variables, through the use of affective education programs was very weak."[44]

Yet schools continue to expand the use of these programs in the name of a "mental health" curriculum. Many schools see self-esteem boosting as their major objective. But the programs they use have little positive results and waste valuable educational time.

In fact, there is evidence that affective programs can have a negative effect on student behavior. Researchers at the University of Southern California compared groups of students placed in affective drug education programs with students in control groups who received no drug education. They found that, compared to the control group, those receiving the affective program increased their use of tobacco by 86.4 percent, increased their use of alcohol by 42.4 percent, and increased their use of marijuana by 74.2 percent.[45] The researchers concluded that "no preventive effect of the affective education program was observed. By the final post-test, classrooms that had received the affective program had significantly more drug use than controls."[46]

This represents a classic case of crisis acceleration. In an effort to curb a problem, schools unwittingly accelerate the problem. While some educators may argue that trying something is better than doing nothing, in the case of affective education programs just the opposite is true.

Doing nothing appears to serve students better than putting them through these programs.

These programs also have the effect of creating what one psychologist refers to as "the omnipotent child": the child who believes he or she is all-powerful, able to make his or her own decisions about crucial behavior issues. As long as the child feels comfortable with his or her decision then it is the right decision. When we tell students that drug use or violent behavior is a decision, we are inadvertently telling them it is an option. Yet surveys of students have found that young people often do not have the proper foundation to make good decisions. They lack the conscience or the will to do the right thing.

Cheating and Dishonesty

The Josephson Institute of Ethics conducted a survey of almost 3,243 high school students regarding their values, attitudes, and behaviors and concluded "there is a hole in our moral ozone and it seems to be getting bigger."[47] The survey found that 33 percent of the high school students polled admitted to having stolen something from a store within the last twelve months, 21 percent admitted to having stolen two or three times, and 11 percent admitted to having shoplifted four or five times within the last year.[48] According to the survey almost seven out of ten (69 percent) of the high-schoolers admitted to lying to a teacher at least once in the last year. One third of the students said they would lie on a resume, job application, or in a job interview to get the job they want. Sixty-one percent of the high school students admitted to having cheated on an exam during the school year. More than 25 percent admitted they had cheated at least four times during the year.[49]

Since 1969 the percentage of students using some kind of cheat notes during an exam has increased from 34 percent to 68 percent in 1989. The percentage of students who let others copy their work went from 58 percent to 98 percent during that time.[50] The Josephson Institute survey dramatically illustrates the decline in ethical behavior among students from 1969 to 1989 in the following areas:

	1969	1989
"Lied to parents about school."	55 %	70 %
"Signed parent's name to an excuse."	26 %	48 %
"Taken books from a library without checking them out."	8 %	19 %
Agrees with the statements:		
"Honesty is the best policy."	82 %	60 %
"Crime does not pay."	89 %	65 %
"To succeed in business requires some dishonesty."	32 %	45 %
"People who cheat can't be trusted."	61 %	41 %
"A cheater at school will cheat on the job."	72 %	43 %
"Most people in the USA are honest."	49 %	24 %
"Sooner or later cheating will be discovered."	83 %	75 %

The survey revealed that students' unethical conduct was, for the most part, not because of lack of moral conscience but from lack of ethical will. For instance, 78 percent of high-schoolers say they believe that cheating is always wrong, yet 61 percent admit to doing it at least once in the last twelve months. Forty-five percent admit to doing it two or three times, and almost 10 percent admit to cheating ten times or more in the last year. Michael Josephson writes, "Many teens recognize that academic dishonesty is wrong, yet they speak of cheating as if it is a behavior that is out of their control."[51]

Controlling Behavior

In many schools paddling a student for violating behavior codes is no longer an option. It has gone by the wayside as schools move on to more "progressive" forms of therapy—discipline such as peer-group counseling, social-worker family intervention, or the schools' version of "time-out"—suspension. In Arkansas, junior high school principal John Heath was included on a statewide list of child abusers by state "human-services" investigators for paddling one of his students. A court found no evidence to substantiate the charges of abuse, but this poor man's name had to remain on the state's list of child abusers for three years without further incident.[52] One small victory for misbehaving students. One small erosion of educators' authority.

"Progressive" school board members in Dade County, Florida, voted to prohibit *parents* from spanking their children on school grounds. The board president assumed the role of the mother of all children in the school when she said, "It sends the wrong message to students to allow or even encourage parents to come to school and hit their children."[53] In Arizona the state board of education tried to ban all corporal punishment in schools for children under sixteen years old. When the state's Attorney General informed the board that such a ban exceeded their authority they modified it to require written parental permission before spanking a student. Of course, the effectiveness of swift punishment and the administrative hassle of trying to obtain written permission will mean that most schools will not administer paddlings to misbehaving students.[54] This trend in schools' diminishing use of corporal punishment is following the trend in parenting styles. In the thirty years between 1962 and 1992 spanking has dramatically fallen out of favor with parents and time-outs and "grounding" children have grown in popularity.

In 1962, 59 percent of parents spanked their children. By 1992 that figure had dropped to only 19 percent. Parents' use of time-outs during those years rose from 20 percent to 38 percent, and groundings rose from 5 percent to 14 percent.[55] It is common for educators and school officials who abhor corporal punishment to refer to it as hitting, striking, and even abusive; they insist it teaches children to be violent themselves. Yet no one refers to time-outs as abandoning, alienating, and rejecting the children and teaching them to emotionally alienate others.

What is not accepted by corporal-punishment opponents is that there is good violence and there is bad violence. As commentator Dennis Preager points out, the Holocaust was ended by violence; slavery was stopped by violence. Good violence is distinguished from bad violence by its relationship to a moral standard it is used to enforce. But when society struggles to define moral standards, it has trouble defining appropriate punishments. In an interview with *Education Week*, Thomas Lickona, a professor of education at the State University of New York, pointed out that many teachers "think the way to start a lesson on values is to say there is no right or wrong answer."[56]

It is hard to justify spanking when you cannot distinguish right from wrong. Not that spanking is necessarily the best discipline practice, but its ban by official government edict serves to illustrate a loss of nerve.

In many instances, absent a religious foundation for morals, educators resort to some kind of self-interest to admonish children to do the right thing. Lessons on honesty or kindness emphasize how good the students will feel for having done the right thing. In the end, this kind of lesson may be sending the same message as the "value-neutral" lessons currently being taught in so many classrooms. "Do it because it feels good" is only one step away from "If it feels good do it."

However, there are hopeful signs for the future of character education. There are a growing number of educators and policymakers who recognize the importance of teaching students moral standards as schools once did. It's just unfortunate that this has become such a glaring necessity.

To address violence in the classroom some schools are beginning to deliberately teach virtues to students. No longer relying on open-ended discussions that may leave the student ambivalent about what is right, these schools aggressively teach kindness, empathy, cooperation, and respect.

Some urban schools have tried to use metal detectors and specially equipped doors to curb the presence of guns in their schools, but this approach has not worked well. New York City schools developed a security system in which all side doors to a school automatically locked and guards used stationary and hand-held metal detectors to interdict weapons. The program was supposed to cost fifteen million dollars and be installed by the beginning of the 1991 school year. By the beginning of 1994 not a single school had a properly operating system, and the cost had ballooned to thirty-eight million dollars. Apparently part of the problem was that students quickly learned how to break the security doors.[57]

Metal detectors seem to be a waste of money in stopping the flow of weapons through a school or in curbing violence. "Little scientific evidence exists to suggest that such devices have any effect on reducing the presence of weapons or the number of violent incidents on school grounds," writes one reporter. Ronald Stephens of the National School Safety Center points out that there is no evidence that metal detectors have any effect at all.[58]

One pilot program designed to reduce violent behavior in children shows some signs of success. Project FAST Track—FAST stands for Families and Schools Together—works with low-income parents and their first-grade children. The children learn socially acceptable kinds of group interaction and also receive academic tutoring in phonics-based reading. Their mothers are paid fifteen dollars per week to participate in the sessions and also to attend parenting classes that focus on reducing the severity of their discipline practices and increasing the warm, nurturing responses children need. Researchers who designed the program caution that while behavior problems have been reduced in early grades the real test will come when the children reach their teenage years.[59]

The Public Orphanage Expands

Creating and managing alternative schools for students expelled from regular schools is a growth industry in the 1990s. Many school districts have taken a "get-tough" attitude toward disruptive students and have, in essence, created schools that are one step away from juvenile detention centers. Students with behavioral problems need tight structuring of their day. "These kids want discipline; they want to know what to expect," says Barbara McDonnell, executive director of the Colorado Department of Human Services.[60]

The Corpus Christi, Texas, school district started an alternative program that emphasizes academic performance and intensive discipline and self-control. The students wear uniforms. They cannot wear jewelry. They must walk the halls between classes in silence and cannot talk to one another during class except during class discussions. At all times they carry a chart on which teachers can mark their infractions of the rules at anytime during the day. Their studies include a special focus on citizenship and leadership as well a regular schoolwork. As they abide by the rules and do well academically they earn small privileges such as being able to talk and store their books in a locker. They are in school from 8:00 A.M. until 5:00 P.M. and perform community service work after regular classes.[61] For students who wash out of alternative schools, the only other options are the streets or the jails.

What happens when the programs designed to relieve parents of parental duties fail in their efforts? Where will the children go when the orphanages no longer work? Public policy must focus on restoring families, not relieving them.

From Schools to Orphanages: A Quick History

PUBLIC EDUCATION, by definition, is not only conducted for the
general public but works to create a general public. That is, it both
serves individual families that are part of the public and shapes what
we mean by a public—or common—society. Public education promotes
a governmentally approved body of knowledge. It allows the government to determine what an American should and shouldn't know. The
recent move by those in the national education leadership to define
national "outcome" standards for each academic discipline is only the
most recent attempt at greater government control. Schooling in
America hasn't always been as it is now.

The History of Competing Values

During the colonial period of our nation's history education was
primarily for learning to read the Bible and understand laws. It served
the purpose of promoting Protestant beliefs and social order while con-
veying social status.[1] With the birth of the nation many American leaders
believed it was necessary that the primary purpose of education change.
They saw the need for education to unify the new nation and provide
social order through teaching strong patriotism and good citizenship.[2]

In other words, education should serve national rather than merely personal ends.

Thomas Jefferson strongly advocated a very limited form of public education. He emphasized the freedom of the individual to shape his or her own political beliefs, and he believed education should only focus on reading and writing. This, he believed, would give the individual the ability to make his or her own political judgments in the marketplace of ideas. Jefferson's famous quote regarding newspapers reflected this view when he said, "were it left to me to decide whether we should have a government without newspapers, or newspapers without a government, I should not hesitate a moment to prefer the latter. But I should mean that every man should receive those papers and be capable of reading them."[3]

Jefferson held the view that education should create a "national aristocracy of talent" rather than an aristocracy based on family or property as in Europe.[4] Education, he believed, was the means of selecting that talent through the process of performance.

Schooling before the American Revolution and well into the mid-1800s was done at home and in small, neighborhood schools. There was no state-run, compulsory education. Yet Americans were a highly literate people. For instance, in just the ten years from 1813 to 1823 Sir Walter Scott sold five million copies of his novels. This would be equivalent to selling sixty million copies today! And the type of writing the early Americans read was complex sentences that many would find difficult today.[5] An Illinois newspaper in 1842—ten years before the first state passed compulsory education laws—wrote with great concern that only 94 percent of the population was literate. We would jump for joy if that were true today.[6]

Despite the success of the existing system of education, the view that emerged in the early 1800s and eventually became the force behind the public—or "common"—school movement was that education should be a unifying activity promoting the basic principles of a republican form of government. Unlike Jefferson, the common-school reformers saw the school "as an equalizer rather than a selector" in society.[7]

The Common School

In the 1840s Horace Mann, often considered the father of public education, became the most influential force in the common-school movement. Industrial and social changes during this time created class conflicts Mann believed could be averted through the homogenizing effects of common schools teaching a common ideology.[8] Mann once explained his move from being a lawyer to being an educator by writing, "Men are cast-iron; but children are wax."[9] Mann believed social problems should be solved through shaping the behavior and attitudes of children in school.

He and other education leaders borrowed heavily from the Prussian model of education that was developed in Europe just a few years before. Prussia was a militaristic and industrial power that wanted to create obedient soldiers and workers who were subservient to the almighty state. Structured schools emphasizing conformity, order, and state-approved knowledge were the key, and American educators in the 1800s jumped on the idea.

Common-school reformers encountered conflicts over what political and religious ideas should be taught in schools. In response to these conflicts they advocated only instruction in the basics of American government and nondenominational religious values. However, what common-school advocates viewed as basic teachings on republicanism tended to promote the ideologies of their political party while the nondenominational religious content resembled mostly the liberal Congregationalism most of the reformers practiced.[10] David Reynolds and Fred Shelly observe that: "Textbooks used in the common schools of the nineteenth century were filled with references to Whig and Federalist heroes with only scant and usually critical references to Jefferson and Jackson."[11]

In other words, the common schools became a way to impose those ideas of the people in power on all families.

Conflicts Surrounding the Common School

What made the common-school movement different from previous ideas about public education was the advocacy of a direct connection between schools and government policies for solving social, economic, and political problems. Not only did the schools, in this view, have the mandate of carrying out the intentions of social engineers, they needed state agencies to control the direction of local schools.[12]

There were staunch opponents to this view of schooling—people who valued freedom of thought over conformity. As one historian put it, "the nineteenth-century conflict over state education was an ideological clash of the first order."[13]

Opponents held that state-run education posed a basic threat to liberty, that compulsory-education laws were immoral, and that an "approved" curriculum would amount to indoctrination in government-endorsed views. A leading opponent of the common-school movement, Joseph Priestly, wrote that education should not be primarily about preserving social order but should be about producing "wise and virtuous men."[14] He was right, of course, but in the end, school reformers had convinced the American people that a common school shared by all citizens was vitally important in shaping and stabilizing society.[15] Liberty was too risky. Centralized control seemed safer.

One reason that people accepted the idea of common schools was because of the massive influx of immigrants during the mid- to late-1800s. Irish immigrants arrived in America in droves starting as early as the 1830s. Approximately ten million immigrants from eastern and southern Europe flooded the country between 1880 and 1914. By 1910, 20 percent of all American workers were immigrants.[16] Controlling the masses became paramount.

As cities grew rapidly, educational leaders saw the need for schools to keep children out of mischief as well as to educate them to be effective workers in America's growing industries. Lawmakers enacted compulsory-education laws and expanded the role of schools. In 1870 American schools enrolled 6.5 million students. Within ten years that figure more than doubled to 15.5 million. The average length of the school year also increased from 132 days in 1870 to 144 days in 1900 and 157 days by 1915.[17]

Compulsory attendance, however, caused tensions with many Catholic immigrants who objected to being forced to attend schools that promoted Protestant views and to learn from teachers who read from the Protestant Bible in class. They created private schools to escape "the system."

The justifications for public schools during this time were largely the same as justifications today. In 1919 Ellwood Cubberly wrote in support of public education that compulsory common schools were necessary to prevent and reduce poverty and crime, provide better workers for business and industry, reduce tensions between social classes, assimilate immigrants, and prepare citizens to exercise their right to vote.[18] Sound familiar? Reformers were concerned over the rise in Catholic immigrants and also in uneducated citizens who would not appreciate America's democratic republicanism, ill-mannered and criminal youth, and the alarming rate of illiteracy (which we would consider nothing to be alarmed about today).

As schools expanded their role to take on these social responsibilities, it became necessary to reduce the amount of local control and increase the amount of state control. In this way the social mission of the schools could be better directed and coordinated.

What Happened to Local Control?

Gradually, toward the turn of the century, control of local schools began shifting from politically appointed boards to professional educators. This shift was completed in all major school districts by 1920.[19] Prior to this, schools were run by elected officials or political appointees in school districts that serviced smaller neighborhoods. This created schools that responded more attentively to local needs because the schools were managed by local businessmen and politicians. Unlike today's school boards, these boards managed the schools' curricula and teachers' qualifications, as well as building programs and taxes. Parents and citizens who had a concern over the schools had only to contact neighborhood board members to find redress for their grievances. The absence of state licensing of teachers or state-approved textbooks and curricula meant it was not yet necessary for parents to make pilgrimages to state capitals when they had local concerns.

Around the turn of the century, however, true local control came under attack. For instance, in Ohio lawmakers passed a 1913 bill that reduced urban school boards from between thirty and forty members representing specific sections of the city to only seven members elected citywide in nonpartisan elections.[20] In Philadelphia in 1905 the city board was reduced from 115 representatives to only 24; this group no longer represented small neighborhoods of the city but the entire city.[21]

This new arrangement made it nearly impossible for boards to represent specific neighborhood needs. Candidates for school board needed more money to campaign and could not focus on the needs of their neighborhood. The job of supervising education shifted to educational specialists. Cities began to restructure schools to follow a corporate model, with teachers being the workers, superintendents and principals being the managers, and school boards being the board of directors. The boards, then, were reduced to approving or disapproving what the professional educator/manager designed.

For the last 150 years public education has been on a steady march away from local control. The centralization of teacher licensing by state agencies was mandatory in forty-two states by 1933.[22] Over the years state departments of education have continually grown to control the functioning of local school districts.

The Federal Government Gets Involved

Increasingly, the center of educational discussions and decision making shifted to the nation's capitol as the federal government expanded its role in establishing educational agendas. The federal government became more involved in education when, in 1957, the Soviet Union launched the satellite Sputnik I. Congress's response to the communist threat was to pass the National Defense Education Act of 1958. Eisenhower asked for and Congress passed legislation that provided funding to states for increased testing and guidance of students who could excel in school. Federal funds were also allocated for grants to states for the hiring of more mathematics and science teachers, for purchasing equipment and materials, and for promoting foreign-language training.[23]

This marked the first attempt by the federal government to give funding to states for specific educational programs. It was a direct attempt by national leaders to meet specific governmental interests through specific public school programs. National political leaders bypassed educational experts and local communities in order to control what was to be taught in schools.

Only seven years later, in 1965, President Johnson signed into law the Elementary and Secondary Education Act as a part of his war on poverty. This provided new and markedly increased federal funding for education.

The federal government was now thoroughly committed to not only promoting education but *directing* it as well. Regarding the thrust of the federal government's involvement, education historian Joel Spring comments that:

> The basic thread was planning for the use of human resources in the national economy. In the 1950s, under pressure from the technological and scientific race with the Soviet Union, emphasis had been placed on channeling talented youth into higher education. In the early 1960s, the emphasis shifted to providing equality of opportunity as a means of utilizing the poor as human resources.[24]

This marked the federal government's first real efforts to address the social needs of families through public education policy. The next thirty years saw a rapid expansion of government involvement.

In 1976 President Carter created the U.S. Department of Education in exchange for the political support of teachers' unions. Its role is to collect data on education, give grants to influence the direction of education, and act as a catalyst for shaping America's educational future.

This new influx of money to education and the increased emphasis on measuring and studying progress created a growth industry among educational think tanks, researchers, and program developers. As politicians became more involved in shaping education agendas, the power of education experts increased through their role as advisers and lobbyists.

The shift away from true local control to a system that serves the interests of the state has caused all kinds of community strife. The philosophical split that is at the root of much of this conflict involves the question of who is responsible for the education of the child. The history of American education is the history of a shift from education as a family or neighborhood function to education as a government function. It is a shift from personal liberty to state-approved knowledge.

Collisions with the Family

It is impossible for schools to reach real consensus on the purposes and processes of education. Benjamin Franklin once wrote, "It would be well if [students] could be taught everything that is useful, and everything that is ornamental: But art is long, and their time is short. It is therefore proposed that they learn those things that are likely to be most useful and most ornamental."[25] Of course, the conflict comes in determining what is most useful and most ornamental. Is sex education, for instance, most useful and if so, what is the most useful way to teach about sex? Or what about tolerance or multiculturalism or self-esteem or death education or any one of a dozen controversial subjects?

Educators justify forging ahead on these topics despite the controversies because they see the many family and social problems they feel compelled to solve. However, this concern is nothing new. It is a theme that resonates with every generation. Each generation believes its society is worse than those previous. By the late 1800s the expansion of the schools' agenda into areas that were traditionally the domain of families was justified by concern then that the family was "collapsing or failing in its duties" and in need of school intervention![26] If that were the case, what would the reformers of that era say about families today?

Families living in cities in the latter part of the nineteenth century were burdened by harsh working conditions, crowded and poor living conditions, crime, alcoholism, and other stresses associated with urban life. School leaders saw this as an opportunity for education to step in and solve these problems. The schools for the most part during this time, however, still reflected a Protestant and nationalistic orientation. Government involvement supported a value system that was, for the most part, conservative. And school "intervention" to solve family's problems was tiny compared to today.

It was not until the 1960s and the increased liberalization of education combined with the massive intervention of government that conservatives became alarmed in large numbers. By the 1980s this alarm had grown into heated conflict. The tide had turned. Schoolteachers no longer read from the Bible or led the children in prayer; religious holidays were censored from classrooms; schools used value-neutral courses to teach sex education; internationalism was replacing nationalism; books containing profanity and questionable morals were added to reading lists for their "relevance"; homosexuality was being touted as a legitimate sexual alternative; gender-neutral family roles were emphasized; and educational leaders began talking about cradle-to-grave state education. Conservatives had had enough. It was time to fight back.

Clashes over Selection of Materials

PARENTS OF 230 STUDENTS in Juneau, Alaska's, public schools kept their children out of school for one day as a protest over the school's refusal to remove an objectionable book about homosexuality. The book, *Daddy's Roommate*, deals with a young boy's visit to the home of his recently divorced homosexual father and the man's gay lover. It puts the living arrangement and homosexuality of the father in a positive and natural light.

Parents pulled their children from school after three parent-teacher committees met and decided to retain the book. The publisher confirmed that there have been forty attempts by parents in districts around the country to remove the book.[1]

This kind of battle illustrates how the political nature of education undermines school/family relations. The political ideology of wanting to expand the public acceptance of homosexuality is driving, in the above case, the inclusion of *Daddy's Roommate* in the curriculum. Rather than simply have the debate over homosexual rights go on in the marketplace of ideas in the adult world after graduation, schools are increasingly attempting to shape students' thinking on the issue before they ever reach adulthood. When parents object to this form of manipulation, educators entrench and defend themselves as the guardians of freedom while they stigmatize parents as censors.

The school officials' commitment to imposing a liberal ideology on students is so powerful in this example they are willing to ignore the voices of families of 230 students in a system that only has a total enrollment of 5,400 students. It is ironic that educators often speak of conservatives as guilty of attempting to impose values on schools. Clearly in this example quite the opposite is true. While claiming that this "exposure to diversity" is necessary for learning how to think rather than what to think, quite the opposite is true. Students aren't learning how to think; they are graduating with an ingrained assumption about diversity—an assumption that is often in conflict with their parents' views. To many educators this is progress.

Parents often focus their concerns on what materials their children are reading. If the parent objects to the book, many educators cry censorship. Cases of challenges to books used in schools abound each year. The challenges tend to cluster around similar themes: books that dwell on witchcraft and the occult, graphic sexuality or homosexuality, profane language, and lack of respect for authority. In most cases the school district rejects the parents' request to have the book removed.

In Evergreen, Colorado, an elementary school principal pulled books from a recently added "young adult" section of the school library.[2] He did so after several parents complained that the books were not age-appropriate, contained too many references to drug dealing, and had too much foul language and violence. Immediately "freedom-to-read" defenders attacked the administrator's action as a terrible case of censorship. These people did not argue that the parents were wrong about the contents of the books. They did not debate the literary value of the books. Instead they feared what they perceived to be the bigger issue: a school allowing conservative parents to influence reading selections at all. What was once called *discernment* is now called *censorship* by many in the public school system. In other words, the real issue is political, not educational.

All across the country books have been challenged as inappropriate reading material for children. But consider the titles of challenged books: *Devils and Demons; Unnatural Talent; The Charming; The Headless Cupid; The Witch Grows Up; Stars, Spells, Secrets, and Sorcery; Curses, Hexes, and Spells; Servants of the Devil; The Restless Dead;* and *The Devil's Piper.*[3]

Three of the most challenged books of the 1992–1993 school year were by the same author, Alvin Schwartz. His challenged books were, *Scary Stories to Tell in the Dark, More Scary Stories to Tell in the Dark,* and *Scary Stories 3: More Tales to Chill Your Bones.*[4] Educators are apparently unconcerned about the increase in stories that deal with dark and devilish themes. They are instead more concerned about parents' objecting to their children reading scary stories at school.

Studying the arguments of the two sides in book disputes reveals that each party is concerned over vastly different issues. Parents who object to these books are concerned over the educational content of the material while the educators in these cases are most concerned over the political ramifications of allowing parents to influence curriculum. In other words, while educators should be most concerned about education, too often they are more concerned about power and professional respect.

When Teachers Censor

That the real issue is about power is evident when the censorship runs the other direction—when the school or educator wants to ban something. In these cases professional autonomy supersedes the issue of censorship in the minds of educators. For instance, professional educators rarely question why the school librarian for the most part has sole authority to select or censor any book from the library. The librarian enjoys the position of being able to impose his or her values on all the students. The answer may lie in the fact that the librarian is a fellow professional educator and as part of the established group within the system is an acceptable censor for them. The parent who raises the child is outside the system, not a part of the profession, and often has a different value system than that which is advanced by the state-run school. Educators who defend their censorship take the ridiculous position that they are selectors while parents are censors.

An example of this selective view on censorship occurred in the Alabama State Textbook Committee. The book at issue was a science book called *Of Pandas and People* under consideration for adoption. It was not being considered as a textbook nor as required reading but as a supplementary source book for science classes. In other words, it would be available, but it would not be promoted. The book focuses on the analysis and comparison of two theories of origins: evolution and what the book refers to as "intelligent design." The book is not conclusive regarding either theory but instead challenges students to use scientific methods of investigation in critically analyzing evidences on origins.

Alabama State Superintendent of Education Wayne Teague attacked the book as "another effort to circumvent some Supreme Court rulings that bar religion from public school classrooms."[5]

However, the book does not refer to God, church, creation, or the supernatural. It was, in fact, written to conform to the U.S. Supreme Court's guidelines on teaching origins.

The publisher offered the selection committee a list of endorsements for the book from scientists from Yale, Texas A&M, Oxford, and Princeton. But in the end, due to the political pressure demonstrated by the state's education department, the publisher withdrew the book from consideration. One member of Alabama's textbook committee, former high school teacher and textbook writer Norris Anderson, resigned over the unfair way in which the public hearings were conducted concerning *Of Pandas and People*.[6]

Educators typically claim they are guarding schools from radical minority dogma being imposed on schoolchildren. However, regarding evolution the education establishment's opinion is a strikingly minority one. The vast majority of Americans hold either a strict creationist view or a centrist view. According to a Gallup poll reported in *U.S. News & World Report* 47 percent of all Americans believe "God created man pretty much in his present form at one time within the last 10,000 years." Another 40 percent believe that "man has developed over millions of years from less advanced forms of life, but God guided the process, including man's creation." Only 9 percent of Americans hold to the view that "man has developed over millions of years from less developed forms of life. God had no part in this process."[7]

It is not for lack of education that Americans believe that God was involved in man's origin. The survey also found that only 16.5 percent of college graduates held to a naturalist view while 54 percent held a centrist position and 25 percent were strict creationists. That is, 79 percent of college graduates believe that God was the Intelligent Designer behind man's origin. Hardly a minority view point!

Power, Not Education

In this instance and numerous others the professional educational establishment does not hesitate to censor any view it deems to be inappropriate. The ultimate issue is not about education nor about representing a wide diversity of views. It is about preserving the power of the professional establishment. It is not merely about the advancement of the state's power. It is about consolidating and perpetuating the power of those people in education.

For instance, in the 1980s Congress passed the Equal Access Law, allowing students to form religious clubs in public schools that permit other noncurricular-related clubs. There is no compelling *educational* reason to bar students from doing this. However, many school officials resisted the establishment of these clubs on political grounds. Here was an example of the government passing a law that expanded individual freedom and the education establishment resisting it.

It was not until the Supreme Court finally ruled that such religious clubs on school campuses were permissible that many schools gave in. Still, other school officials felt so strongly about their political stance that they closed down all noncurricular clubs rather than allow a religious club to be established. This action served no educational purpose, but it does show the extent to which the professional educational establishment will go to assert its power.

In a somewhat related situation, a Wauconda, Illinois, school imposed a restrictive policy prohibiting students from distributing even one piece of religious material on campus. On November 2, 1990, eighth-grader Megan Hedges handed out a Christian pamphlet titled *Issues and Answers*. The school principal confiscated her materials and warned her not to distribute any more. Megan and her parents sued the school district, and the court ruled that the school board's policy was unconstitutionally restrictive.

It is hard to imagine what *educational* purpose was served by the school's censorship in the first place. What great harm would come to the school district by a teenager asking her friends to think about God?

In response to the court's decision the school board adopted a new policy that still severely restricted a student from giving religious material to friends. The Hedges sued the school district again, and again the school's policy was struck down. This represented two trials with thousands of taxpayer dollars spent by the district in defending its act of censorship. But the school district would not be defeated. It spent thousands more on an appeal. In the end the district won a partial victory that allowed for certain restrictions.

Three trials, three expensive legal bills for what amounted to nothing more than censorship irrelevant to the academic success of students. In fact, Judge Frank Easterbrook, writing for the seventh circuit court, criticized the district for so willingly censoring student religious speech.[8] It is this type of dogged determination against religious values on the part of many educational leaders that has caused the outrage of conservative Christian parents.

Clashes with Christians

Christian parents have increasingly taken on school districts for teaching values contrary to their faith and for censoring things that are supportive of Christianity. One Christian mother in Buffalo, New York, for instance, was faced with having to defend her second-grade daughter's choice for show and tell. Seven-year-old Mary Rudnicki brought the book *Sam's Special Prize* to school in response to the teacher's request that each child bring his or her favorite book to read to the class. The teacher stopped little Mary from sharing her book with the class and told her the book was inappropriate because it used the word "God" four times.[9]

The irony of this couldn't be greater. If the book had contained the word "God" as an expletive it would have most likely been acceptable. To be fair to this teacher, maybe "God" is taboo for second-graders in her class either as a swear word or to name the Supreme Being, but they need only to wait a few grades. Sixth-graders in elementary schools that have young-adult sections can read all kinds of profanity including the "G word." One study of forty-five popular teen books found profanity in 70 percent of the books.[10]

An English teacher poignantly illustrated the hypocrisy of many schools. She told of being caught without an answer for a group of thirteen-year-old boys when they asked, "Why can't we swear in the halls, when library books have lots of dirty words?"[11]

Parents and even school-board members are frustrated by the continual erosion of moral standards in schools. They are even more frustrated when their attempts to include biblical values in schools are attacked by civil liberties groups. These liberal groups have created paranoia among citizens and educators about Christian involvement in schools.

Christians who get elected to school boards are often branded as part of the religious right. Michael Hudson of the liberal organization People for the American Way (PAW) labels conservative Christian activists as extremists who are out of the mainstream of American thinking.[12]

A growing trend that promises to continue throughout the decade is for groups like PAW and the teachers unions to counter Christians running for school boards by labeling them "stealth candidates." These are, according to their accusers, candidates who hide their real agenda until they get elected to school-board positions. This clever label shifts the issue away from what a candidate says and on to the issue of who he or she associates with. Since, by definition, you cannot identify stealth candidates by what they say, you can only recognize them by their associations.

Instead of the McCarthyite question of the fifties: "Are you now or have you ever been a member of the Communist Party?" the question for school-board candidates in the nineties is, "Are you now or have you ever been a member of a fundamentalist or evangelical church?" If the candidates answer yes they are immediately suspected of being stealth candidates.

In February 1993 People for the American Way met with one hundred liberal organizations in Washington, D.C.—including the National Education Association, the American Library Association, and the National PTA—to discuss how to combat any challenge to public schools from conservative organizations. They explored ways to share resources and work together to stop conservative parents.[13]

The trend is that conservative Christians are being seen as enemies of public education by those in power. This is because the real issue of the educational elite is not merely educational; it is about self-preservation and the advancement of their vision for society. It is my experience that Christian parents would prefer not to have to criticize the school and do not want to compete for power within the system. Their actions are a response to school leaders' imposing new values on Christian children already in the system.

An objective analysis of new programs in schools will reveal that the educational establishment has been imposing changes such as condom distribution, profane literature, liberalized social studies, and self-esteem courses tinged with New Age ideas, while eliminating traditional practices such as Christmas concerts. Consider the following:

- Four hundred parents and concerned citizens turned out for a meeting at Catawba Heights Baptist Church in Belmont, North Carolina, to protest a proposed school program called "Odyssey." A bitter battle with the school district ensued as the parents complained the school was imposing immoral values on students.[15]

- Parents all across the state of Georgia protested a twenty-four-member state advisory panel's recommendations for new sex-education courses. Among other things, the panel recommended that the definition of a family not merely be "those members related by blood, marriage, or adoption." Instead, they wanted to include people living together out of wedlock and homosexual couples who have children. The panel also recommended that children in sixth grade be taught about condoms. It also wanted homosexuality to be taught in such a way as to eliminate negative stereotypes.[15]

- Virginia abandoned its proposed outcome-based education program after parents effectively criticized it for promoting instruction in "correct" values and self-esteem instead of sticking to academic achievement.[16]

- Voters in Littleton, Colorado, rejected the district's move toward outcome-based approaches when they elected three conservative candidates. The conservatives' two-to-one victory was especially significant in light of the incumbents' backing by the educational establishment, which included an open letter signed by fifteen school principals denouncing the conservatives.[17]

- Over two hundred Christian high school students met for a Bible study club on the lawn of their high school in Fountain Valley, California, because school officials would not allow them to meet in a classroom. After months of emotional negotiations with students and parents, the school agreed to abide by the federal law that allows for such student-sponsored activity. Why the school attempted to ban the student club for *educational* reasons is unclear. Only a liberal *political* reason makes any sense of the school's violation of the students' freedom of association and freedom of speech.

Conservative Christians have become the most organized and most vocal opposition to the education establishment. Churches in each school district of the country have become the new hub for activist parents working to protect their children from the heavy hand of Big Nanny. Often these groups are made up of less than a half a dozen parents in a church, but their lobbying of school boards and letters to the local newspaper can create shock waves in a district. When a conflict erupts over a sex education course or an outcome-based curriculum the problem is too often unresolvable through dialogue because both parties have very different agendas.

Clash of Agendas

The experience of former Secretary of Education William J. Bennett illustrates the very different agendas that exist between parents and the educational elite regarding public education. He tells the story of the time he participated in a panel discussion on the direction public education should take in the future. Speaking on the topic, "What do Americans want from their schools?" Bennett outlined the very straightforward agenda for schools that he consistently heard from parents across the country when he asked them: "First, teach our children how to speak, write, read, count, and think correctly. And second, help them develop reliable standards of right and wrong that will help guide them through life." Parents, he pointed out, wanted these things taught in the context of a basic education of math, English, history, and science.

Joining him on the panel were chief state school officers—nationally recognized and influential leaders in education. When they outlined the purpose of schools they talked of teaching students to function well in an "increasingly interdependent world" and appreciating diversity and exhibiting tolerance. None of the members of the prestigious education elite mentioned anything about reading, writing, and math.[18]

This same problem of differing agendas is reflected in a report on "Teacher Education for the Twenty-First Century" published by the American Association of State Colleges and Universities. This group represents 375 institutions and 30 state systems of higher education—an impressive body of educators. The publication did refer to creating literate and technically competent students. However, the educators emphasized the "very different" needs of students in the future. These included the need to be highly adaptable to change, comfortable with diversity, and globally aware. It also advocated the need for schools to "intervene in the lives of children at much earlier ages" to help students prepare for preschool. Schools, in their view, needed to become community centers with evening parenting classes and teams of professionals who could "assess, diagnose and prescribe" various social services to students and their families.[19]

The state of Ohio offers another example of this expanded agenda of schools. The Work and Family Life Program is used in Ohio public schools and in school districts throughout the country. Students spend six semesters (two years) dealing with courses in personal development, resource management, life planning, nutrition and wellness, family relations, and parenting. During this time they are evaluated on 412 nonacademic competencies including how well they:

- Assess self-esteem of self and others.
- Describe parenting skills needed to foster human development and foster caring relationships with infants and young children.
- Identify ways to take responsibility for living in a global environment.
- Identify factors to consider when selecting clothing.
- Use comparison shopping skills to select housing.
- Evaluate environmental impact of food purchases, preparation, and disposal.
- Analyze factors influencing mate selection.

- Analyze psychological and social factors affecting food choices.

- Resolve family conflicts about food choices.

- Recognize impact of food choices on environment and global community.

- Analyze gender expectations and divisions of tasks in relationships.

- Respect rights, feelings, and needs of family members.

- Develop strategies to effect change in society for the benefit of families and children.[20]

One political cartoonist captured the frustration of many in the general public regarding public education's social agenda when he pictured two schoolboys sitting outside the principal's office. One boy was explaining to the other why he was in trouble: "I got caught learning math and science while my teacher assigned studies in gay homelessness and American socioeconomic imperialism!"

Clearly there is a clash of basic agendas between many parents and many education leaders over the purpose of education. While many parents want schools to stick with imparting a fundamental education, many school leaders want to expand the responsibilities of schools to include every aspect of not just a child's development but his family's as well.

I say "many" when referring to both parents and educators because there are also parents who want the schools to take on these roles traditionally reserved for the family. They have grown accustomed to considering the government as a member of their extended family. True freedom is a scary thought to them. It carries with it too much responsibility.

On the other hand, not all teachers agree with the new agenda of the schools. In a recent survey of two thousand teachers it was found that 67 percent of them were concerned that new academic reforms would lead to schools' being rewarded for "figuring out how to get their students to test well but not necessarily learn more."[21] While teachers I have spoken with privately express resentment and frustration with the direction of their schools they hesitate to say so publicly for fear of professional repercussions.

Clash with Teachers

Teachers who encounter opposition to what they are teaching now have a crisis hotline they can call for support. The Center for the Expansion of Language and Thinking started the hotline in 1992 to give "victims" of censorship a place for advice and comfort. The hotline consists of a network of four hundred teachers across the country who are "on call" to lend support to a beleaguered teacher in their area.

A drama teacher in Tucson, Arizona, used the hotline when she ran into problems over a production of *The Shadow Box* by Michael Cristofer. The play includes two homosexual characters and offensive language. Parents were not the only ones who objected to the play. In fact, school administrators and fellow teachers were the teacher's earliest critics. The teacher called the hotline and, as she put it, then "understood the monster I was dealing with. . . . Censorship is a traumatic experience."[22]

Her statement reveals a big part of the problem. Describing the restraining influence of good taste as a monster shows just what a mess we have. While this example could be dismissed as just the poor judgment of one teacher, the existence of a hotline to support her poor judgment tells us a lot about the misguided visions some educators have for public education. It is one more symptom of a public school system at war with itself—the *public* part of public schools is pitted against the school part.

Clashes between parents and educators are on the rise, mainly because the range of issues over which they conflict has expanded. As schools add more "progressive" changes to their missions, battles with parents have increased. For instance, fights over sex education date back to the early 1960s. Back then the issue was simply over whether there should be sex education or not. Today, just within the subject of sex education the fights have multiplied into conflicts over AIDS education, condom distribution, on-campus health clinics, homosexuality, the definition of the family, and lessons on inappropriate touching, sexual abuse, and sexual harassment. Each one of these issues can constitute a separate battle within a district. And frankly, districts bring the trouble on themselves.

As parents have gotten more involved with school policies, programs, and curriculum issues, areas of conflict have mushroomed as well. Districts find themselves entrenching against criticism over required reading lists, textbook selection, school plays, classroom videos, curriculum standards, religious holiday policies, Halloween celebrations, guest speakers, self-esteem courses, whole language methods, cooperative learning techniques, gifted and talented programs, drug and alcohol courses, guidance counselor activities, and tests or surveys that intrude on family privacy.

School officials try an array of tactics to fend off or contain criticism. One method is to isolate the critic and immediately place the issue into a bureaucratic process called the review committee. This has largely proven to be window dressing for public consumption. It has the appearance of being responsive to the parents' concern without actually changing anything in the school. The vast majority of challenged materials that go through this process are recommended for retention rather than replacement.

In Anoka, Minnesota, parents were concerned about new sex-education material for the schools. One meeting at Coon Rapids Senior High School drew nine hundred parents. A review committee was set up. A parent who sat on the committee later commented, "I have served on many committees in my professional life, yet I have never served on a committee which was as closed and controlled as was this one."[23]

She complained that though the most controversial aspects of the sex-education material in question dealt with sodomy, homosexuality, and abstinence, committee members were not allowed to discuss the parents' arguments against these subjects as they outlined in their formal complaint form. The committee chairwoman kept tight control on the proceeding. Though it was a public meeting no tape recorders were allowed except for a recording made by the district that could only be heard by committee members. Two parents not on the committee wanted to meet for coffee with two teachers on the committee to discuss the issues but were rebuffed. "Oh, no, we're not supposed to talk between meetings," said one teacher. Two parents that sat on the committee later referred to the meetings as "rigged, in essence, a sham."[24]

Another method used by school districts to counteract criticism by parents is to quickly hold a public meeting supportive of the school district's actions. An Orange County, California, school district used this approach when one of its school-board members and many parents complained about outcome-based education testing being implemented in the district.

The district held an information meeting in which both sides of the issue were to present their case. However, before this took place district administrators orchestrated a three-hour filibuster of praise for the district—a love fest for itself. Scores of teachers took to the podium to talk about the many wonderful things their schools were doing. Late into the evening the meeting turned to the original controversy. The two educators presenting the district's case spoke first and at length. Finally, near midnight, the conservative school-board member was allowed to speak. By this time many parents had gone home. The vast majority of the audience that remained were teachers who supported the district. Yet the district could rightly claim that a public airing of the problem had been done.

Teachers Strike Back

Educators have not been sitting idly by as parents criticize schools. Teachers—or more precisely—teachers unions have responded with vehement attacks against parents who oppose the current barrage of changes in public schools. Local teachers union representatives routinely denounce active conservative parents as extremists, fundamentalists, fascists, antidemocratic, racists, sexists, and homophobes. Union leaders conduct meetings for teachers and hand out lists of enemy organizations. These "black lists" include organizations such as Focus on the Family and Campus Crusade for Christ. They even include the entire Evangelical Free Church denomination.

I attended one such meeting in our local school district and found the union's presentation easily fell apart when just a few teachers asked rather simple but probing questions. For all the talk among educators about the need for critical-thinking skills for students, I found this meeting demonstrated great emotion but scant critical thinking. Conservatives were stereotyped; their concerns were simplified to appear moronic; a union videotape that was clearly propagandizing was touted as an unbiased presentation of fact. Fortunately, in this situation, many of the teachers in attendance appeared unconvinced of the union's assertions.

Nevertheless, union representatives relentlessly preach their message in districts around the country: "Anyone who opposes anything happening in public education is an enemy of public education."

The California Teachers Association president, D. A. Weber, criticized school-voucher supporters' efforts to put an initiative on the ballot by saying: "There are some proposals that are so evil that they should never even be presented to the voters. We do not believe, for example, that we should hold an election on 'empowering' the Ku Klux Klan. And we would not think it 'undemocratic' to oppose voting on legalizing child prostitution."[25]

To equate school choice with child prostitution and empowering the Ku Klux Klan reveals the kind of hate the education establishment has for those who oppose them. The union reportedly spent eighteen million dollars on their campaign to defeat this California initiative.

Despite the union's vigorous opposition, school-choice initiatives have exploded across the country. While proposals vary in each state, the basic idea is to give parents vouchers from the state worth a certain amount of money for their children's education. This voucher can then be applied to a school of the parents' choice. Some proposals include private schools as possible recipients of state funds while other proposals include only public schools.

In the five-year period between 1987 and 1992, laws were passed in thirteen states giving parents the right to send their children to public schools outside their local school districts.[26] Between 1990 and 1994 voucher proposals were put forth twenty-four times in eighteen states.[28]

Privatization of education in some form is an idea whose time has come. Efforts to privatize public schools will continue throughout the decade and reflect the mounting crisis facing the current system. Calls for choice in education are a symptom of one of the underlying problems with public education—it is moving further and further away from parents as it seeks greater political domination.

Rather than respond to this change in public desire, the National Education Association and the American Federation of Teachers met in 1993 with leading educators from 120 nations to form Education International with a major focus of fighting the "worldwide phenomenon" of privatizing education. Mary Futrell, former head of the NEA, is Education International's first president while the current head of the NEA, Keith Geiger, will serve on its board of directors.[28]

It is worth noting that while American businessmen try to respond to what the market wants, the leaders of American educators try to resist the desires of the market. While the businessman tries to find out what the consumer wants and then makes the product accordingly, the leaders of the education establishment, in essence, say to the consumer, "We have a warehouse full of our product, and if you don't like it and if you want to go to a competitor we'll spend our energy trying to stop you." And they have a formidable army to do it.

The National Education Association has fifty-two state-level affiliates and around thirteen school-district branches. It boasts the largest membership of any union in the country: 2.1 million teachers. *Forbes* magazine estimates the local, state, and national income of the union to be $750 million.[29] This forms a powerful special interest group lobby from the nation's capitol on down to each legislative district in the country.

In its national conventions the NEA passes resolutions to consolidate its power and fight anyone who opposes the direction it is moving education. For instance, in its 1991 convention in Miami, teachers resolved to push for legislation that required that parents who try to escape public schools by home-schooling their children must have teachers' certificates, be licensed by the state, and teach only curricula approved by the state.[30]

The union works vigorously to build and protect its political power in Washington, D.C., and in state capitals. State union affiliates are among the top, if not *the* top, contributors to legislative campaigns. The California Teachers Association, for instance, was the top contributor to campaigns in that state in 1990 with $1,056,815 going into the coffers of politicians.[31]

The power of the union, both through its money and through its ability to put manpower behind or against a candidate, creates a climate of intimidation among many politicians. This, the union hopes, will keep its agenda for public education safer.

The union's political influence can come in extremely sophisticated forms. For instance, union officials started three years *before* the 1990 census was even conducted to use the results for favorable legislative redistricting. State union leaders were trained at NEA headquarters in Washington, D.C., on how to use advanced computer systems to lay out their states' legislative districts and then convince politicians to conform to their desires. In Indiana the state union actually bought a computer the size of the government's so union staff could, as they put it, "mirror what the government had" regarding the census and redistricting.[32] The strategy was that union-friendly legislators would then parrot the union's gerrymandering desires.

Mickey Ibarra, the union's political-advocacy director for government relations, put it this way: "In some respects, it became a game of who had the biggest computer. We encourage our folks not to look at it that way. [Redistricting] primarily is a game of raw political power."[33]

The impact of this was to rearrange legislative districts and increase the number of Democratic voters in Republican strongholds in Indiana and throughout the country.

In Colorado the teachers union teamed up with People for the American way to root out any conservative school-board candidates who might have links to the "religious right." PAW distributed a ten-question survey to candidates to see if their answers matched any positions held by the religious right.[34]

In this way the union could attack someone, not on the merits of his or her position on educational issues, but on even the most remote link to other groups.

In Florida, where the teachers lobby is powerful, a bill died in committee that was designed to stop teachers from using students as political activists. The bill would have forbidden teachers from requiring their students to write to government officials expressing the *teacher's* viewpoint. The bill was formulated after legislators received thousands of letters from children in support of more taxes for education. One senator complained that in some instances kids were forced by teachers to "copy verbatim from the board" a sample letter that supported the tax increase.[35]

In this climate of tension between the establishment and the public, it is little wonder that educators report poor relations with parents! A recent survey found that 40 percent of teachers said they intend to leave the profession because parental support and cooperation are so low. Only 25 percent of educators polled described their relations with parents as satisfying.[36]

Could it be that schools have so insulated themselves from meaningful parental involvement that they have, in the end, hurt themselves? As the school seeks a different agenda and greater autonomy, it is quite understandable that parents will disconnect from positive involvement. There is little incentive for parents to be involved in a system that allows them no real control. Not only do schools allow little authentic parental control; they also insist on controlling more of the child-rearing tasks. The professional educators' combination of shunning parents' influence on school policy while simultaneously relieving them of their parental responsibilities will naturally result in demotivated parents. An organization that only allows its participants the choices of conforming or leaving will see only apathy and desertion. So while educators complain that parents are not involved enough they are doing the very things that ensure parental noninvolvement.

The only thing that will bring about greater parental involvement in supporting local schools is increased opportunity for authentic participation. The current structure of schools has resulted, with few exceptions, in the professional insiders setting the agenda and controlling the discussion. Parents' only recourse in this situation is either to do nothing for the school or become a political activist seeking to pressure the school into listening. Either way, the school loses. It either loses important parental input through apathy, or it wastes valuable parental energy in political battles when it could be tapped in positive ways.

As the teachers unions seek greater power and autonomy, they will continue to fight any person or group who threatens their growth. The increased conflicts between liberals and conservatives over educational content will create even greater resentment toward public schools.

By the end of this decade, barring any success with voucher programs, the public-school establishment will remain embroiled in conflicts with parents and conservatives. New talk about having parents participate more in local school governance will do little to resolve conflicts that arise from state and national agendas. Unless we turn away from the aggressive agenda to turn our schools into orphanages, schools will continue to have battles each year.

These orphanages, like any "family," want to raise their children with certain values. Since it is these values that bring on battle after battle, let's take a closer look at what they are. The good news is we don't have to continue the way we are going. But I'm getting ahead of myself. Let's look first at the way we are going.

Part Two
The Values of the Orphanage

To assume that education is exclusively about cognition and learning and that teaching is exclusively about imparting academic skills represents a very narrow view of both learning and teaching.

William E. Davis,
Professor of Education,
University of Maine at Orono

8
Sex Education and School Clinics

I F SCHOOLS REPRESENT the "new American family" seeking to raise our children, we need to look at their "family values." Let's start with one of the most controversial.

Sex is one of the hottest issues in education. Why? Because sexuality issues embody fundamental values about relations between people, religious convictions, and parents' control over their children's intimate development.

Several years ago I was asked to speak about sex education at the National Association of Physician Assistants conference. I entitled my speech, "Sex Education and Other Adult Sexual Hang-ups." Instead of joining in the familiar chorus of educators decrying conservative parents who don't talk to their kids about sex, I spoke about how students hadn't changed that much over the years but adults certainly had. While biologically the average age of a girl's first period has lowered from 14 a century ago to 12.5 today, the most radical changes have been in how adults deal with sex.[1]

Adults are the ones making television shows and movies more sexually explicit. I don't think you could find one teenager writing to Hollywood executives complaining that television and movies are not sexually explicit enough. Adults are the ones who are creating sexually alluring advertising. Adults are the ones writing the sex-education courses.

Adults are the ones promoting homosexual "sensitivity" training in schools. Adults are the ones turning incidences of ill-mannered childhood taunting on the playground into landmark cases of sexual harassment.

In short, it should come as no surprise that children are becoming more sexually aware and active. They are only responding to the messages the adults in our society give them. The problem is that while many parents recognize this problem, they are often unwilling to take responsibility for the healthy sexual education of their children, and too many educators want to wrench this responsibility from them. Their aim is to create a society whose views on sexuality are properly progressive and "liberating."

Pop Culture's Curriculum

A *Newsweek* article entitled "The End of Innocence" captured a major part of the problem well. Children of any age can watch sex slaves interviewed on daytime talk shows and sing along to "Me So Horny" or "I Want Your Sex" on the radio. They can see men and women posing seductively in magazine and newspaper ads. They see ads for condoms and warnings about AIDS. Their heroes are scantily clad pop singers and movie stars who proudly talk about their decision to have a child out of wedlock.

Hollywood is eager to exploit sexual issues and change sexual attitudes in America. For instance, each year television shows include more homosexual characters and themes. The Gay and Lesbian Alliance Against Defamation actively lobbies studios to include positive portrayals of homosexuality. Many of the shows that include homosexual characters use a predictable format: The main character initially is repulsed by the homosexual's conduct but by the end of the show has "matured" in his or her thinking and accepts the alternative lifestyle.

Television provides a powerful curriculum for anybody, especially children. A curriculum is basically any specially formulated system for teaching, influencing, or informing someone's mind, attitude, and behavior. This is a fitting description of television. Former U.S. Secretary of Health and Human Services Louis W. Sullivan once pointed out that in a typical year "the three major networks will depict more than ten thousand sexual incidents, 93 percent of them outside marriage."[2]

Against this outside pressure to sexually stimulate children and youth there are forces within public education that are seeking to change children's views on sexuality. Educators' and policymakers' reasons for pushing for these changes fall into two major categories: ideological and pragmatic.

Many public-education leaders are ideologically committed to breaking down traditional attitudes regarding sex. They believe sexual freedom for young people is a right. They advocate contraceptive education and the installation of school health clinics as a means of helping students exercise their sexual rights. In their mind the issue is to extend the students' sexual rights while also teaching them the responsible use of those rights through contraceptive education and refusal skills (until the children determine they are ready for sex).

There are also educators who are motivated more by pragmatism than ideology regarding contraceptive education and school health clinics. From this view—used more widely today—educators simply point to the rise in teenage (and even preteen) sexual activity and assert that "something" must be done to stem the negative effects of this promiscuity. They point to the breakdown of family authority and the flood of sexual messages from the media as the reasons for schools to take on this responsibility since they are the only remaining institution capable of making a real impact.

Despite the obvious hardening of children's attitudes toward sexuality, sex education "experts" complain that children don't think about sex enough. Debra Haffner, executive director of the Sex Information and Education Council of the United States (SIECUS), laments that only 10 percent of children receive comprehensive sex education at every grade level. SIECUS wants schools to include instruction in sexual behavior, fantasy, homosexuality, and masturbation.[3] Susan Wilson, a sex-education trainer in New Jersey, complains that, "We hardly ever talk to teens about necking and petting and admiring your body and maybe massage."[4]

School-Based Health Services

Imagine the school of the not-so-distant future: Your child will be able to hand a note to her seventh-grade English teacher excusing her for a medical appointment she made that morning. She walks down the hall to the clinic, which is only two doors away from the principal's office. There she receives her contraceptives, and she asks a few questions about sex with her fourteen-year-old boyfriend. The nurse listens and answers in a nonjudgmental tone.

"How are things going in your family?" asks the nurse. The child responds that she is having trouble relating to her mom. The nurse suggests the girl make an appointment with the school counselor, and she may want to attend a group counseling session tomorrow after school where she can express her feelings about her mother. Throughout the school year the girl is reminded of the clinic's free dental service, mental-health services, and (just in case the contraceptives fail) prenatal care and childcare services for teenage mothers. The rest of her family can enjoy free access to the clinic as well. Mom and Dad can attend parenting classes in the evening and even have a social worker do home visitation to intervene in domestic problems. Welcome to the school of the future—not just in inner-city neighborhoods but in middle-America, too.

There is increasing support for schools to be, as Joy Dryfoos calls them in her book *Full-Service Schools,* "surrogate parents."[5] Schools will reorganize to provide for all of the child's (and in some schools the family's) physical and emotional needs. Schools will also have the responsibility for employment services, childcare, parent education, social-worker case management, recreation, nutrition and dieting programs, family planning, mentoring, cultural events, welfare, community policing, "and whatever else may fit into the picture."[6]

There were only 12 school-based health centers in existence in 1980. By 1986 that number had grown to 62, and by 1990, there were 162 clinics.[7] There are now almost 500 school-based clinics in place in middle and high schools serving about 750,000 students, and their numbers will increase rapidly as public education's social agenda expands.[8] Dryfoos, an influential clinic advocate, suggests there should be at least 16,000 clinics in schools in order to meet the growing need.[9]

During the 1980s there were heated battles over having school-based health clinics. Conservatives rightly feared that the clinics' "family-planning" programs would mean greater acceptance and support of teenage sexual activity. That battle was largely won by the education establishment. As Dryfoos writes:

> The 1992 Gallup Poll reported that 77 percent of respondents favored using the public school buildings in their communities to provide health and social services to students,

administrated and coordinated by various government agencies. . . . A 1993 sample survey of North Carolina registered voters showed that 73 percent believe that health care centers offering prevention services should be located at high schools—with the strongest support from African-Americans and from eighteen- to thirty-four-year-olds and with no differences in gender, religion, or parental status. More than 60 percent favored providing birth control at the centers.[10]

A 1993 Gallup poll indicated 65 percent of public-school parents surveyed wanted condoms distributed at school, although 23 percent of those would require parental consent. It is worth noting that in the 1992 Gallup poll, 68 percent of respondents favored condom distribution while, to the question of whether such availability would increase teen sexual activity, 40 percent said it would. However, their overriding concern was protection against unwanted consequences of the students' behavior.[11] Another example of pragmatism prevailing over standards.

The school-based clinics of the future will be "one-stop shops" for all the student's *and* family's needs. The local school will become the headquarters from which every conceivable welfare program will be launched into the community. In short, families will be encouraged to rely on the government (in the form of the local school) for an incredibly wide array of services. Socialized medicine will be delivered in America through public schools.

The education establishment's push for schools to be "one-stop" social service centers will not occur without the potential for a variety of unintentioned effects. We have seen earlier that government programs to fix a problem often accelerate the problem or at least create another equally menacing problem. Here is what could lie ahead for public schools as they expand their roles to include school-based health and social services:

1. *Teenage sexual promiscuity will increase.* Even school clinic advocates such as Joy Dryfoos admit that "systematic evidence that school centers improve health outcomes is still somewhat limited."[12] More specifically, a careful study of the research on school-based clinics reveals there is little empirical evidence of substantial success in reducing

teen sexual activity. In fact, one research team investigating the impact of birth control-oriented pregnancy-reducing programs found that teen pregnancies rose. They reported that "instead of the expected reduction in teenage pregnancies, greater adolescent involvement in family planning programs was associated with significantly higher teenage pregnancy rates."[13]

There are no studies to indicate that condom distribution in schools reduces teenage sexual activity.[14] The presence of clinics and the staff's openness and acceptance of teen sexual activity will send a powerful message of lowered expectations for teen behavior. This will translate into a self-fulfilling prophecy.

For instance, in New Jersey, where K-12 sex education is law, 67.7 percent of teenage pregnancies in 1980 involved unwed mothers. Sex educators helped to increase that figure to 84 percent by 1991.[15] Douglas Kirby, a researcher for ETR Associates, a health-education firm in Santa Cruz, California, has been studying the effectiveness of sex-education courses for a number of years. He finds that sexual knowledge does not translate into responsible sexual conduct. What research has found is the value of families in shaping and controlling teenage sexual behavior. Studies have found that parental discipline and supervision (more so than parent-child talks about sex) had a great effect in reducing teen sexual activity. Teenagers who have less parental supervision, or daughters who are raised in single-parent homes, or teenagers from less-religious families tend to have higher rates of teen sexual activity.[16]

2. *Condom distribution to students will place them at greater risk of HIV infection.* Recent research indicates it is wrong to assume that since condoms are 87 percent effective against pregnancy they have the same effectiveness against the spread of HIV. Researchers at the University of Texas Medical Branch at Galveston report that condom effectiveness in preventing the spread of HIV ranges from as low as 46 percent to as high as 82 percent.[17]

3. *Children will be socially and emotionally "emancipated" from their parents.* Providing for the health and welfare of children is the primary function of parents to children. School social services will reduce this

function and in many cases replace it. As teachers, school nurses, and guidance counselors look after these needs, parents' sense of responsibility will be reduced. The irony of this is that clinic advocates are motivated by their concern over troubled families. Many of these proponents insist that these services should reach out to the parents as well. However, parental involvement usually means, above all else, support for the services and increased dependence on them. Parents who already feel overwhelmed by the demands of making a living will be all too cooperative in relinquishing this responsibility, and thus the schools will have accelerated the crisis of the breakdown of family relations.

Children also will be emotionally separated from their parents with such programs as Learning About Family Life, developed by Rutgers University Press. It has the effect of encouraging children to see the school as the safest place to discuss intimate issues such as sexuality. For instance, the curriculum describes a conversation about genitals between a boy and his teacher in which the boy says, "We never talk about that stuff in my house." To which the teacher responds, "Well, you can talk about it in school, Brian."[18]

A brochure called "Let's Talk About Sexuality" given to students in Seattle-area schools tells students how to discuss sexuality with their parents. It instructs students, "Be patient. Remember, your parents are still learning too," and, "Listen to your parents. Practice being a good listener and let your parents know you care about their opinions."[19] One avenue for emotional emancipation opens when schools portray to children that their parents are still learning about sexual issues and that their moral views are merely opinions.

4. *Sex-education courses will increasingly add sexual pleasure to the curriculum along with sexual information.* When sex educators speak of emphasizing abstinence, they often mean abstaining from sexual *intercourse*, not sexual experiences. Masturbation, sexual fantasy, and playfulness are being integrated in courses from kindergarten through high school.

For instance, the K-3 program Learning About Family Life teaches little children, "it's OK to masturbate," and the "clitoris is a small sensitive part that only girls have, and sometimes it makes you feel good." If a man were to say such things to little girls in the park he could be brought up on charges of child annoyance or obscene activity.[20] In a public park it is harassment, in a public school it is education.

Teachers using this program describe sexual intercourse in a section on love and affection this way: "The woman and the man place the penis inside the woman's vagina."[21] While the children are taught that this is an expression of love and affection, they are not taught that it should be in the context of marriage.

The most influential sex-education organization, SIECUS in 1991 distributed twelve thousand copies of its guidelines for sex education to school districts. The guidelines urge schools to teach children ages five to eight that "both girls and boys have body parts that feel good when touched." Children nine through twelve are to be taught that masturbation is a common way to experience pleasure, and SIECUS urges high schools to teach students that "sharing erotic literature or art, bathing/showering together" are normal components of sexual relationships.[22] This last bit of advice sounds more like it's from a course on rekindling your romance than from a high school health curriculum.

Kindergarten students in Irvington, New Jersey, get to listen to their teacher read aloud about how babies are made:

> "When a woman and a man who love each other go to bed, they like to hug and kiss.
>
> "Sometimes, if they both want to, the man puts his penis in the woman's vagina and that feels really good for both of them.
>
> "Sperm come out through the man's penis. If one tiny sperm meets a tiny egg inside the woman's body, a baby is started. . . ."[23]

Do kindergartners really *need* to know this?

5. *Conservatives will increasingly be ridiculed and sidelined by the education establishment.* Sex-education "experts" frequently refer to abstinence-based programs as "fear based." If parents don't want homosexuality discussed, they are accused of being homophobic and

hatemongers. Conservatives are often put down and sidelined in debates as only wanting to impose their morality on everyone.

Ironically, it is the sex-education establishment that so desperately wants to impose moral views. Debra Haffner, the director of SIECUS, for instance, declares her moral position emphatically: "Adolescents who are capable of forming healthy sexual relationships must be supported."[24] President Clinton's national AIDS policy coordinator, Kristine Gebbie, addressed a conference, saying, "As long as we couch our messages around sexuality in terms of don'ts and diseases, and don't recognize [sex] for the positive thing it is, . . . we will continue to be a repressed Victorian society that misrepresents information, denies sexuality early, denies homosexuality—particularly in teens—and leaves people abandoned with no place to go."[25] By definition the one bringing the new morality to the classroom is the one doing the "imposing." Liberal sex educators seem incapable of recognizing that they are imposing their views on others.

6. *Children and youth will become more sexually aggressive.* Students are desensitized by a lot of what they see on television and in movies and what they hear on the radio. Our society seems bent on stripping children of innocence and pushing them into sexual aggressiveness. In the future students will be further desensitized to sex because of explicit sex education. New sex-education courses will consciously strip away childhood modesty. An increasing number of students will see sex as a casual activity on par with going to the movies, something that is expected in a "normal" dating life.

Programs now exist that justify early and explicit sex education on the grounds that "sexuality is a part of daily living, as essential to normal functioning as mathematics and reading."[26] The result may very well be more incidences like that of the "spur posse" in Lakewood, California. The "posse" was a group of boys ranging in age from fourteen to eighteen who gave each other points for each girl they had sex with. Two teenagers were alleged to have had sex with a ten-year-old girl.[27]

Problems of sexual aggression in children and teens have already increased dramatically. In Montclair, New Jersey, two fourteen-year-old girls were gang-raped three times by boys, including some in the seventh grade. Michael D. Resnick, associate professor of public health and pediatrics at the University of Minnesota, surveyed thirty-six thousand teenagers for a study on adolescent violence and concluded, "We're seeing earlier onset of behavior that used to be reserved for late adolescence, then it was early adolescence and now it's late childhood."[28]

To strip students of their modesty, some schools resort to burlesque. Chelmsford High School in Massachusetts sponsored a speaker to give an assembly on AIDS awareness. Her presentation, entitled "Hot, Sexy, and Safer," included having one student pull a condom over the head of another student and asking a student chosen from the audience to make an "orgasm face." The school administrator defended the presentation stating that an "overwhelming number" of students liked it.[29] Students' enjoyment and adult approval of this officially sanctioned lewd conduct is just one more indication of sexual callousness.

At Monroe High School in Monroe, Washington, students made clay models of male and female genitalia as part of their health class. The Planned Parenthood guest speaker who initiated the activity defended herself by saying that only student volunteers molded the genitals. A few years ago a student would be summarily disciplined for such antics; now he or she can get extra credit. Thus is the progress of civilization.

Fortunately, there were students with enough decency in both the AIDS burlesque and the crafty health class to leave the room in disgust or later complain to officials. But while students protest the assault on their decency, the adults press on, undaunted.

Schools teach refusal skills to help students ward off unwanted sexual advances. However, the operative word is *unwanted*. Greater social acceptance of teen sex will create greater incidences of *wanted* sexual advances. And it will create a climate wherein adolescents feel more free to make sexual advances.

The president of the Essex County parent-teacher council, Kathleen Witcher, complained, "It's very popular now for teenage boys to stay overnight at girls' houses. There are no sanctions."[30]

7. *Full-service schools will cause more of the public to abandon support for public education.* This is the irony: As schools try to do more for the

public they will actually push more of the public away. This may not be true in lower socioeconomic communities where welfare programs are a more common part of the social fabric. There, parents may welcome the added convenience of expanded social services. But large numbers of middle-class parents will resent the increased welfare programs of the public schools. This resentment will most likely occur even if their local school is not full-service. Public education in general will suffer the scorn of these parents who will react negatively to the schools' Big Nanny syndrome and will eventually look for other educational alternatives. This, of course, won't be true of all middle-class parents, but the numbers will be large enough to significantly erode support for the schools.

Sex education strikes at the heart of parental responsibilities, and it is odd that parents would delegate the teaching of such an intimate subject to virtual strangers. Educators defend sex-education courses by pointing out that most parents don't talk to their children about sex. But these same educators do little to encourage parent-child communication on the matter. Sex education is simply yet another family prerogative that government has encroached upon with an aggressive agenda. Unfortunately, too many parents are relieved that somebody else (anybody else!) besides themselves is broaching the subject with their kids.

9
Feminism and the Classroom

I N E D E N P R A I R I E , M I N N E S O T A , a six-year-old girl was taunted and insulted by boys using "sex-related" terms while riding the bus to school. She complained, and the district promptly disciplined the boys, removing one from the bus for a week and banning another from riding the bus for the entire year—a reasonable, some would say severe, punishment. This was not enough, according to the U.S. Department of Education. It ruled that the *district* discriminated against the little girl because it did not treat the misconduct specifically as sexual harassment. In other words, the girl was a double victim: once at the hands of the boys and once at the hands of the district! Welcome to the feminist movement as it manifests itself today, where children's misconduct becomes revelations of male oppression of women.

"Perhaps no sociocultural factor is having a greater impact on children and schools than feminism," writes education consultant Myron Lieberman.[1] The feminist movement, as defined by Lieberman, is seeking to "eliminate gender differences that arise from discriminatory treatment of women." In practice this often means defining traditional family roles as discriminatory, regarding homemakers as less than "liberated," and promoting the view that women are victims of male-dominated society. It affects children from the textbooks they read to the lifestyle and career choices they make, and from the way boys and girls interact to the absence of mothers at home when children finish school each day.

My concern over what has happened with the women's movement is not about women becoming doctors, lawyers, or construction workers. It is about what has happened to mothers in America. At one time in our nation's history the term *pro-family* meant encouraging mothers to stay home to devote time to their children. Today, to be pro-family in most feminist circles means encouraging mothers to leave their children with someone else so they work all day just like their husbands. That's considered good, and that's what's wrong.

Feminism has made great strides in infusing its ideology into school curriculum and textbooks. It has literally changed the way teachers teach and schools function. A majority of elementary teachers routinely use more stories about the heroics of girls than of boys. Textbooks rarely show women in domestic roles and instead show them having careers. Sex-education classes no longer segregate boys and girls but instead teach them together to break down any sexual timidity they might have toward one another and thus, supposedly, send the ever-important message that boys and girls are equal even in sexual immodesty. In general, the woman's role is to be changed, demand the feminists, and schools comply.

The result has been an expansion of opportunities for women and an astounding increase in women taking advantage of those opportunities. As Charles Sykes writes, from the 1960s to the 1990s "the number of women elected to public office tripled; the number of women lawyers and judges multiplied more than twentyfold; the number of women engineers rose from 7,404 to 174,000. One-third of MBAs are earned by women (as are half of the nation's law degrees and a quarter of the medical degrees). Fully half of entry-level management jobs are now filled by women, as are half of the officer and manager spots in the country's fifty top banks."[2]

Since 1970 this has increased the wages of women aged nineteen to thirty-four but at the same time it has created stagnation and decline in the real wages of men of that age. In fact, women's gains in *opportunities* to work have translated into their need to work to help sustain the family.[3]

Yet, despite the impressive gains in education and the workplace, feminists complain that not enough is being done in schools to create "gender equity." For instance, the American Civil Liberties Union filed a civil-rights complaint against the administering of a test to award National Merit Scholarships. The ACLU's charge is that the testing must be unfair since 60 percent of the semifinalists and finalists are boys even though boys make up only 45 percent of those taking the test. The complaint stems from the outcome of the test rather than the content of the test.[4]

To understand how feminists can see tests, textbooks, and even teaching techniques as *biased* you need to understand the extent to which they broaden the use of the term. A book published for teachers and administrators, for instance, gives the following examples of gender bias in teaching:

> Uses of language in ways that privilege the masculine over the feminine (e.g., "he," "you guys," "mankind," etc.).
>
> Fostering an atmosphere of competitive individualism where achievers are recognized and the noncompetitive students are disadvantaged.[5]

Myra and David Sadker have devoted an entire book, *Failing at Fairness: How America's Schools Cheat Girls*, to the issue of gender bias in schools. They claim that having students call out answers in class is an "open invitation for male dominance" since boys tend to respond more than girls. They also claim "male dominance" on the playground, where boys take up more space to play their games than do girls. Their research is so biased toward a feminist slant that even positive news about girls is given a negative spin. For example, they acknowledge that in general girls get better grades and receive fewer punishments, and they refer to girls as "the elementary school's ideal pupils." However, in their eyes this is not so good because that means girls are not getting enough attention or challenges and female passivity is being reinforced by the schools.[6]

An interesting fact missing from their research is pointed out by education researcher Jacquelyn Eccles, a University of Michigan psychology professor. She found the biggest gender difference between boys and girls in school is that boys get yelled at more than girls.[7] An article written in 1981 highlighted a study that found low-achieving boys were reprimanded eight to ten times more frequently than were girls. This finding got twisted and used by feminists to popularize the myth that boys call out answers eight to ten times more than girls. Between 1992 and 1994 no fewer than twenty-nine major newspapers and national magazines reported this myth as fact.[8] If these findings were reversed—that girls were reprimanded more than boys—the feminists could have a field day with a new form of victimization.

The fact is, girls have consistently outperformed boys in reading and writing proficiency, and the gap has *widened* slightly over the years. In 1971 seventeen-year-old girls scored twelve points higher than their male classmates on standardized reading tests. By 1990 the gap had slightly widened to thirteen points. Regarding writing achievement, in 1984 seventeen-year-old girls were twenty-two points ahead of boys, and by 1990 they were twenty-four points better at expressing themselves in writing.[9]

In math and science, high school girls have made *more rapid improvement* than boys. From 1970 to 1982 both groups' science scores dropped twenty-two points.[10] What is interesting is that girls rebounded better than boys. From 1982 to 1990 girls improved by ten points, and boys only improved by four points. Consequently, the gender gap from 1970 to 1990 closed from a seventeen-point difference to an eleven-point difference.

In math a similar phenomenon occurred in which girls made more rapid gains than boys after both experienced slight declines. The net effect was that while there was an eight-point gap in 1973 there was only a three-point gap in 1990.[11] Hardly a trend worth complaining about.

Feminist cries of bias and oppression also seem odd in light of research on how females are portrayed in textbooks and elementary readers. Dr. Paul Vitz of New York University did a study of bias in textbooks for the U.S. Department of Education. In examining a majority of history textbooks used in schools he concluded that recent American history is portrayed "in terms of three issues or themes: minority rights, feminism, and ecological and environmental issues. In every case the pro position is presented as positive; the opposition is never given any serious treatment."[12] In studying forty textbooks used in grades 1 through 4 Vitz found that no book presented "in any form a sympathetic portrayal of traditional sex role models for the contemporary United States."[13] Instead, every picture of a woman showed her as doctor, auto mechanic, a construction worker, a police officer, a firefighter, a mail carrier, and the like while men at work were portrayed in traditionally female-dominated jobs such as telephone operators.

In analyzing elementary readers Vitz points out, "By far the most noticeable ideological position in the readers is a feminist one."[14] In his study he found stories of girls who slew dragons, girls who beat boys in athletic events, and girls who outsmarted boys. He characterized this phenomenon as "Wonder Woman and the Wimp." Even in stories about historical figures, women received greater attention than men. For instance, there were many stories about female aviators such as Amelia Earhart and Harriet Quimby but nothing on Charles Lindbergh and only a one-page story on the Wright Brothers in only one reader. Vitz concludes:

> Some kind of feminist emphasis characterizes approximately 10 percent of the stories and articles in the sample, that is, sixty-five items. . . . As already noted there are no equivalent stories representing traditional concepts of womenhood. Likewise, countless parents wanting clear male role models for their sons will not find them in these books.[15]

In light of all this, it seems odd that feminists complain that schools are hostile and oppressive toward women. Their cries seem like one more ingredient in their efforts to victimize women.

Sexual Harassment

The latest manifestation in feminist victimization is sexual harassment on school campuses. What was once labeled crude and ill-mannered behavior among children has been politically elevated to be on par with sexual coercion of a woman by a male boss at work.

I do not mean to minimize the inappropriateness of demeaning teasing and lewd insults between children at school. When a boy uses foul language or crude gestures at school—especially when directed to someone else—he should be punished. However, *sexual harassment* is a legal term that changes the dynamic of student interaction.

For the feminists it is not enough that boys be punished for misbehavior; they must see themselves as the oppressors of women.

A cottage industry has developed over the study of sexual harassment and the development of programs to deal with it in schools. Nan Stein of the Center for Research on Women developed a seven-day sexual harassment curriculum for the National Education Association. Since the NEA has 2.1 million members its curriculum has the potential of having the greatest impact nationwide. In commenting on sexual harassment to *Education Week*, Stein wrote, "To thousands of adolescent girls, school may be teaching more about oppression than freedom; more about silence than autonomy."[16] Male dominance rather than misconduct is the focus of sexual harassment charges for feminists. However, it is interesting to note that one study of this issue found 76 percent of boys in grades 8 through 11 reported being sexually harassed and slightly more than half of all the girls surveyed admitted to being harassers.

One problem in these surveys and in dealing with the issue is that sexual harassment has taken on a broad definition. Not only does it include demeaning sexual comments such as derogatory remarks about a person's body and physical contact such as snapping a girl's bra or pinching her derriere, it has also come to mean a suggestive look or a boy's "repeated and clumsy attempts to ask out a girl who isn't interested."[17] Locker-room insults between boys or "pantsing" someone (pulling down his gym shorts) is also considered sexual harassment. Even boys' "domination" of class discussions is seen by some as a form of harassment.[18] It is entirely possible that kindergarten boys' talk of getting "girly germs" will be classified as sexual harassment since some civil-rights bureaucrats see harassment as language and conduct "expressing hostility toward someone based on their sex."[19]

As more and more behaviors are labeled sexual harassment by schools, the real issue will become more trivialized. If someone tells me he or she was sexually harassed I *now* ask, "What do you mean by sexual harassment?" whereas before I would automatically be outraged.

There is no doubt a problem exists with misbehavior between boys and girls at schools. As I discussed earlier, both genders are being trained by our society to be more sexually aggressive and casual about sex. They learn to consider their own sexuality and the sexuality of others as having little more mystery and sacredness than eating lunch. One teenager, for instance, in Lexington, Massachusetts, was reprimanded on sexual harassment charges for calling a fellow student a "slut," a "whore," and other sexually offensive names. Though repentant of his actions, he commented to *U.S. News and World Report*, "I was brought up to treat women equally. I couldn't understand what I had done."[20] That is exactly the problem. For this young man, girls held no special place, and he saw nothing wrong with expressing himself to her in the same foul-mouthed way he spoke to male buddies. He was brought up to treat women equally bad. He is an equal opportunity gutter-mouth.

For the sexual-harassment-policy proponents the issue is not so much what is said but what the victim's reaction is. "It is the *reaction*, not the intent, that is important," says Nan Stein.[21]

The lesson the children learn is that sex is not special; only individuals' power over their own body is special. That is why sexual harassment is defined in terms of how the *victim* feels about the abuser's comment more than the actual comment itself. Sexual harassment, then, is seen as attacking or attempting to dominate a woman's power. In such a climate appeals to moral conduct have been replaced with legal prohibitions. Moral power is replaced with political power. Laws and regulations always increase when morals and manners decrease.

Where Feminists Are Leading Schools

The feminist agenda for society will continue to significantly impact public education both directly and indirectly. We can see much of this occurring today.

1. *Textbooks will include more feminist heroes in order to give girls role models of female success.* Though there already is an imbalance in the portrayal of sex roles, more feminist role models will most likely be included. Girls who do not want to pursue careers will feel out of step with the "norm."

2. *An explicit effort will be made to seek female math and science teachers.* Feminists complain that girls do not perform as well in these subjects because there are not enough women role models as teachers of math

and science. Certainly there is nothing wrong with having women in these positions unless it results in discriminating against other qualified applicants simply because they are male.

3. *Classroom instruction will deemphasize competition and emphasize small-group discussions and cooperation.* This is not necessarily only in response to feminist complaints of male-dominated learning environments, but it does coincide with it. Under this thinking classrooms change from promoting individual excellence to pursuing the path most comfortable to everyone's—especially girls'—feelings.

4. *Textbooks will increasingly promote role reversals in showing males in nurturing activities and females in leadership and occupational roles.* Girls will be taught to be more aggressive while boys will be trained toward passivity. More women will reject traditional roles of homemaker and motherhood while more men will reject their traditional role of provider. Self-fulfillment for both sexes will supersede mutual fulfillment through marriage.

5. *Schools will include sexual harassment curricula and policies for all grades.* Already there are programs springing up around the country such as Alice in Sexual Assault Land performed by high school students. In one school, fourth graders analyze how television promotes sexual stereotypes (as defined by feminists) and are taught to write letters lodging complaints to the networks. Sexuality is depersonalized and moves from the private arena to the public. Everyone will be trained to be a victim of harassment.

6. *School health and social services will be expanded to include women's "reproductive rights."* Contraceptive distribution and abortion referrals will increasingly become a part of these on-campus clinics. Children and families will become more reliant on the state rather than on themselves.

7. *More schools will become day-care facilities in order to support working mothers.* Schools will be open to students from 6 a.m. to 6 p.m and will serve breakfast, lunch, and dinner.

To be "pro-women" too often translates into being pro-working-women. For families with children between the ages of six and seventeen the rate of women working rose from 28.3 percent to 73.6 percent from 1950 to 1990.[22] Schools will accelerate the crisis of fragmented families by encouraging students to grow up to be mothers who work full time and, with day care, provide those working mothers the freedom to pursue their careers without being responsible for their children. The schools will have then created a self-perpetuating situation wherein they encourage girls to work full-time as adults, which leads to less maternal nurturing of children, which will require more institutional nurturing of those children, which will require expanded programs for an already overwhelmed system. The result is a self-fulfilling prophecy wherein the once academically oriented school will need to transform to the public orphanage.

10
The New Liberal Arts 101: Multiculturalism

I N ORDER FOR THE NEW surrogate family's members to get along, the public orphanage tries to instill a multicultural value in each child. This is the new liberal arts. A liberal arts education traditionally has meant an education in subjects that make up our general culture. This includes studies in history, languages, philosophy, politics, literature, and the arts. The new liberal arts that are often being taught in many classrooms today, however, are focused on the art of being a liberal. As public education continues to expand its responsibility in creating the "right" society, it gives greater attention to molding the thinking of students toward what it deems right.

Education has always played an important role in shaping what a society believes to be the right way to live. In times past, however, there was greater consensus on what this way of life should be. American society has begun to fragment into more separate and distinct groups. There are ethnic groups that want the school curriculum to be shaped by ethnic issues. There are moral groups—both liberal and conservative—that want the curriculum to be shaped by moral issues. There are political groups—both left, right, and center—that want the curriculum to reflect their political ideology more closely.

A public school can respond to this growing diversity in three ways. One option is that it can attempt to be all things to all people—and find itself mired in continual struggles between competing forces. Another option is that it can narrow the scope of its mission and allow the cultural debate to go on outside the school, not within it. A third option is to give up on trying to deliver a "public" education and instead adopt some form of privatization allowing parents to choose their own school.

As education consultant Myron Lieberman writes, "no curriculum will satisfy the different groups with diametrically opposed views on family issues."[1] How does home economics or health class satisfactorily teach about family issues when we can't agree on the definition of a family?

Even taking into consideration the recent moves within public education for greater variety of structure, the most likely future will not be any of the above options. Instead, state and federal government committees will use "outcomes," "frameworks," and "guidelines" in an attempt to maintain firm control of the curriculum content. This move toward greater government control will occur because public education is seen by many as the one institution that can create some sense of commonality in a society that continues to fragment.

This will continue the tradition of public education working to create a consensus within society. However, what is different from past generations is that over the years curricula and policy formation has been largely captured by liberals promoting their vision of what America should be. It is this drift to the left that has created the new liberal arts.

Thomas Sowell writes that to these educators, "The premier job of schooling is not to impart knowledge and skills, to transmit the culture, to empower individuals, or to produce competent, self-reliant adults. Rather, it is to reconstruct the society around it, a society that in its present form is too gravely flawed for conscientious educators to want to prepare youngsters to live in."[2]

Multiculturalism

The growth of non-European ethnic minorities is a major trend that will continue well into the twenty-first century, and its impact on public education will be significant. Since the 1960s more than 75 percent of immigrants to the United States have been non-European. Hispanics have made up about 47 percent and Asians 22 percent, while blacks have made up 8 percent of immigrants.[3] The Census Bureau reports that one in seven, or 31.8 million, Americans speak a language other than English at home. From 1980 to 1990 people speaking Spanish at home grew 50 percent (17,339,172 people over age five) and represented the largest non-English-speaking group. The ten largest language groups in America are listed below:

Total Speakers Over Five Years Old

Language	1990	Change from 1980
Spanish	17,339,172	50.1 %
French	1,702,176	8.3 %
German	1,547,049	3.7 %
Italian	1,308,648	19.9 %
Chinese	1,249,213	97.7 %
Tagalog	843,251	6.6 %
Polish	723,483	12.4 %
Korean	626,478	127.2 %
Vietnamese	507,069	149.5 %
Portuguese	429,860	19.0 %

European and non-European ethnic groups are evenly split at five each (if you count Spanish as representing ethnic groups outside of Spain). However, if you look at the ten *fastest-growing* language groups between 1980 and 1990 another picture emerges.

Total Speakers Over Five Years Old

Language	1990	Change from 1980
Mon-Khmer	127,441	676.3 %
French Creole	187,658	645.1 %
Hindi, Urdu, and related	331,484	155.1 %
Vietnamese	507,069	149.5 %
Thai	206,266	131.6 %
Korean	626,478	127.2 %
Chinese	1,249,213	97.7 %
Tagalog	843,251	86.6 %

Arabic	355,150	57.4 %
Spanish	17,339,172	50.1 %

No European ethnic group appears on the list, and Asian language groups make up 60 percent of the list (3,559,718 people).[4] It is worth noting that three out of four people who reported speaking a foreign language at home also reported that they spoke English "well" or "very well."

At least one researcher estimates that by the year 2020 the Asian-American population will reach 20.2 million, or about 8 percent of the population.[5] Some analysts expect the Hispanic-American population to become the largest minority group in the country by the year 2014. Already in 1991 Hispanics accounted for 11.8 percent of K-12 students in the country.[6]

Legal immigration has ballooned from around 300,000 per year in the 1960s to around 675,000 per year in the 1990s. Illegal immigration accounts for another 200,000 people per year. In fact, immigration now makes up almost one-third of the total U.S. population growth annually.[7]

Complex Problems for Minorities

Not only do many school districts have the difficult task of teaching students who do not speak or understand English, they also face the range of problems associated with minority students such as high dropout rates, low achievement, delinquency, drugs, poverty, and broken families.

Schools and community leaders have had difficulty providing solutions for many of these problems. In some cases well-intentioned programs have had little or no effect. For instance, the National School Boards Association Council of Urban Boards of Education reported that the segregation of black students today exceeds that of 1970 when busing was seen as a way to create racial integration. In many school districts white families have opted for private education or moved to the suburbs, leaving schools that are predominately minority.[8] In another instance of a failed program aimed at minority students, one study found that media campaigns to encourage black youth to stay in school, avoid drugs, and other positive behaviors have "failed miserably."[9] It went on to reveal that black urban youth have "a closed subculture that encourages dangerous behavior, threatens to ostracize those who do not conform to its views, and appears almost as alienated from its own African-American traditions as it is from the white mainstream."[10]

This problem of negative black teenage peer pressure was also found by anthropologist Signithia Fordham of Rutgers University. She conducted a two-year study of the phenomenon of black students' underachievement and concluded that students felt torn between achieving academically and being accepted by their peers. Many black students viewed the kinds of activities required to succeed in school as "acting white." She commented, "I never believed it would be so pervasive, and so pronounced, and so academically stifling."[11]

New Cultural Curriculum

In response to problems of minority youth, race relations, and the surge in immigrant children, schools have emphasized multicultural education to varying degrees. Within education there are two major views on this issue. The assimilationists believe that studying other cultures is part of a well-rounded education, but they emphasize the blending of cultures into something uniquely American, heavily influenced by western European culture. On the other hand, cultural pluralists see the "melting pot" as a bigoted form of ethnocentrism. They believe that schools should have a "value-tolerant" environment where each group's culture is promoted.

Rod Janzen, professor of social science education at Fresno Pacific College, sees these competing approaches as a contest between absolutism and relativity. He writes, "Americans have historically subscribed to principles of constitutional democracy, which are grounded in the Judeo-Christian heritage. Defenders of this tradition dislike relativistic approaches that encourage individuals in ethnic groups to 'be who they are,' even if being who they are means supporting a divergent interpretation of democratic ideals and practices."[12] This is precisely the problem many parents and educators have with the multicultural movement. The movement often is manifested as a relativistic philosophy in the classroom or simply a liberal extension of the civil rights movement. One leading multiculturalist reflects this when he includes homosexuals, feminists, and disabled people under the multicultural umbrella.[13] Under such a definition multiculturalism is not about ethnic differences; it simply becomes indoctrination in accepting differences—any differences.

In the end, multiculturalism is not only about understanding but about power. Multicultural proponent James Banks reveals that the goal is to "negotiate and share power."[14] Thus, for the liberal, education is an extension of politics. But it is a politics of separatism all the while hoping to unite our nation. As Banks writes, "Teaching from a range of perspectives will prepare students from diverse groups to work together in a truly unified nation."[15] One wonders what we will have left to unify us if our focus is on our disunity. How will teaching sixth-graders in Washington, D.C., to sing a Zulu song called "Prayer for Africa" help American students who are not from Africa and who probably have difficulty finding it on a map? How will having an African Swahili party for third-graders in Rowland Heights, California, bring unity to our nation when four of the students are from Mexico, two of the students are from Korea, and the rest of the class was born in America?

Even something as seemingly objective as science is not immune to the politics of multiculturalism. The National Academy of Science will incorporate a multicultural approach to science by including in its national science standards lessons on Aztec astronomy and number systems.[16] It is hard to imagine how Aztec astronomy will help students learn to be better scientists (though it is easy to see how the *political* feelings of certain pressure groups might be stroked).

The Evils of Columbus

To help students understand issues of power and race, many teachers used the quincentenary celebration of Columbus's discovery of America as an object lesson. These teachers did not focus on the good that came from Columbus's voyages. In fact, many did not focus on Columbus at all. One multicultural teacher-trainer glowingly reported that teachers who took a more enlightened view of Columbus had a very different focus: "[T]he most common response to the question 'What did you do about the quincentenary in your classroom?' was to describe a lesson or project concerning Native Americans."[17] The real lesson for these children was on social injustice, power, and how to take political action to correct it. The questions these students grappled with were "How is the legacy of Columbus connected to today's inequalities of power, privilege, and wealth? How have people resisted domination? How do they continue to resist, and what are the prospects for fundamental social transformation?"[18]

To teach this lesson, one teacher, for instance, had students in a Portland, Oregon, high school commemorate Columbus Day by "invading" other classrooms, stealing teachers' purses, and claiming them as their own. Afterward, the enlightened students led the "invaded" students in discussions on the abuse of Indians by Columbus. The lesson ended with the teacher "offering black armbands to students as a way of demonstrating solidarity with Native Americans' 500 years of resistance."[19]

Multicultural Therapy

A growing trend is for schools of education in colleges to include courses on multiculturalism. In some instances it is hard to tell whether the course is about social science or psychology. For instance, San Diego State University requires prospective teachers to take a course on multiculturalism. The course is designed to have students find out who they are and why they do what they do. "First, you help them understand who they are. Have they ever been discriminated against? What do they know about their culture?" explains the course instructor.[20] One wonders what these prospective teachers really do know about their American culture as opposed to, say, Aztec astronomy. In keeping with the liberal trend in multiculturalism the dean of the college of education at San Diego State says that after effectively infusing schools with ethnically-oriented multiculturalism, she wants to move on to "issues of gender and disability." I wasn't aware that we have gender cultures and disability cultures.

A middle school multicultural program called Project REACH (Respecting Ethnic and Cultural Heritage) uses psychology and sensitivity training extensively. The children are run through activities with names like "You and Your Feelings," "Feelings in a Day," and "The Feelings Bag." All of this is done in the name of helping students understand who they are and how they can get along with people of other races. Unfortunately, so much time is spent on these types of activities the students learn little of what we have in common as Americans.

One frustrated parent wrote to me, "I'm sick of it!" Her son was in the fifth grade and had yet to learn of the Revolutionary War, the Declaration of Independence, the Constitution, or any American president. Yet every year since first grade he had been taught about a variety of minority cultures and the histories of foreign countries. The teacher taught about how other cultures outside America celebrated religious holidays but never taught about how Christmas and Easter are celebrated in America by religious people. The irony of this is that holidays such as Christmas and Easter are unifying events celebrated by a wide variety of ethnic groups. Yet the religious nature of these holidays is seldom taught.

What schools end up doing is miseducating students about holidays. For instance, in Missouri while the Lee's Summit High School concert choir performed the "Winter Holiday" program, the stage was decorated with a Star of David, an Islamic crescent, an Indian thunderbird, and a Christian cross. Are students to conclude that Hanukkah is a Jewish version of Christmas and that Muslims and pantheistic Indians celebrate their holidays at the same time as Christmas? Or maybe they are supposed to learn that Judaism, Islam, Pantheism, and Christianity have an equal impact on American culture.

The Racism of Multiculturalism

It is a form of racist stereotyping to assume that because a student is of a particular ethnicity he will be better served by studying his ethnic history than by studying Western civilization. I find it far more beneficial to study Jewish and Christian traditions than I do to study my ethnic roots in Ireland and Germany. And whether a good idea came from Ireland or Germany means nothing to me. The importance of the idea or value stands head and shoulders above its geographic origin.

Whether an American student is black, Asian, white, or Hispanic, on issues of law, government, religion, literature, reasoning, science, and music he or she is strongly influenced by Jewish, Greek, and

European ideas and traditions. Certainly many cultures have contributed to the world's repository of knowledge. But multiculturalism wants to define people by their race. It isn't interested in the content of someone's character, but the color of his or her skin. I was raised believing that that was racism. Schools deprive students of accessing the benefits Western civilization has to offer through our American culture and institutions when educators supersede our Western heritage with faddish multicultural lessons. As commentator Paul Harvey wrote, our schools' obsession with establishing some cultural identity other than simply "American" is "tantamount to keeping your first wife's picture in your second wife's bedroom."[21] And that can't be very therapeutic for anybody.

Politically Correct Education

The same mentality that gave us multiculturalism also gives us the "anti-bias" speech police. In various states "inappropriate" school mascots are being challenged for their insensitivity. In Wisconsin the attorney general distributed to school districts his opinion that schools with Indian-related nicknames violate the state's antidiscrimination laws. His reasoning was that "the use of an American Indian logo, nickname, or mascot could strengthen a stereotype and create an intimidating or offensive environment that would help perpetuate discrimination." Whether it does this is not the issue. According to this gentleman the possibility that it *could* is enough to censor its use.[22]

Students are asked by the multicultural speech police to now see witches in a more positive light. A group of early-childhood educators in California who are a part of the Anti-Bias Curriculum Task Force wrote a manual for teachers entitled *Anti-Bias Curriculum: Tools for Empowering Young Children*. In it the educators make this "empowering" assertion:

> The Halloween image of the "witch"—old, ugly, wicked, and dressed in black—reflects stereotypes of gender, race, and age: Powerful women are evil; old women are ugly and scary; the color black is evil (a connection that permeates our language). Moreover, the myth of the mean, ugly, evil witch reflects a history of witch-hunting and witch-burning in Europe and

North America—from the Middle Ages through the Salem witch-hunts of the seventeenth century directed against mid-wives and other independent women.

The manual then offers an example of how one teacher named Kay taught children ages four to six in an after-school care program to be more accepting of witches and witchcraft.

> Day 1: Kay asks, "What are your ideas about witches?" "Bad, ugly, old" are the children's unanimous responses. Kay: "Many people do think that. What I know is that the real women we call witches aren't bad. They really helped people." And the teacher then reads the children a story.
>
> Day 2: Kay brings in a number of different herbs: mint, clove, cinnamon, and gingeroot. She introduces the herbs to the children, letting them smell them. They talk about what they think they could use them for, and then Kay tells them briefly about how the herbs have been used to help people.
>
> Days 3, 4, 5, and 6: Kay sets up a number of activities children can choose to do over the next week: a "witch-healer" table, where the children can make their own potions; a tea-making table, where the children can make and drink mint and cinnamon teas; planting herbs; and making collages with herbs.
>
> Follow-up: After a week of these activities, Kay has another brief discussion with the children about witches. "What do you know now about witch-healers?" she asks. The consensus is that witches fell into two categories. Some were bad, some good. So although the activities don't completely change the children's minds, they do stretch thinking by creating a category of "some good witches."[23]

Lest you think this is some fringe group with little impact, their manual is distributed by the National Association for the Education of Young Children, in Washington, D.C.

This same group, which has thousands of preschool and elementary teachers as members, also recommends that Thanksgiving be celebrated by studying the Native Americans so that children "become critical thinkers and not repeat or continue the injustice of the past or present."[24]

Their hypocrisy as anti-bias crusaders is telling, however, when they suggest three ways to celebrate Christmas. According to this group, teachers should either integrate all December holidays from several cultures into an ecumenical mishmash, or they should "do December holidays other than Christmas," or "don't do December holidays at all in the classroom."[25] I suppose they see no bias in being biased against the holiday celebrated by Christians. For them, such blatant discrimination is not bias; it's justice.

The triumph of multiculturalists over uniculturalism is best illustrated by the victory they won in Lake County, Florida, in 1994. There, school-board members voted to install a policy that required teachers to "instill in our students an appreciation of our American heritage and culture such as our republican form of government, capitalism, a free enterprise system, patriotism, strong family values, freedom of religion and other basic values that are superior to other foreign or historic cultures."[26]

This was too much for the teachers union, which sued the district to have the policy repealed. In the end, new school-board members were elected who pledged to erase the "controversial" policy. But why was it controversial? That policy did not say—as multiculturalists claimed—that other cultures were inferior to America's culture. A thoughtful reading of the policy reveals that it says that certain "basic values that are superior" are to be taught. The policy does not require teachers to teach that America is inherently superior. If a foreign culture values the family, capitalism, representative government, and the like, it too has a superior culture to those that don't.

Multiculturalists would have us believe that the only thing worth valuing is the dogma that "all things are of equal value." Such is the recipe for cultural genocide.

11
The New Liberal Arts 102:
Eco-Educators and Global Educators

"SENSITIVITY" IS THE NEWEST, and sometimes it seems highest, ethic in many schools today. Not only are students indoctrinated into being more sensitive to all groups of people but to nature as well.

In at least one school district in Washington children who go through an outdoor education program encounter environmental sensitivity training. While in the woods each child is told to stand next to a tree by themselves and complete this worksheet:

"Activity #1: We Are One with Nature

Directions: Stand facing your tree, with your hands on its trunk. Look at your tree and notice its color, size, shape and height. Look up slowly through the branches to the very top. As you do this just relax and try to see its beauty, feel its strength and as it moves, hear it talk.

Now let yourself become a feeling part of your tree.

Softly, Gently, Quietly.

When you are ready, complete the following: [student is to write an answer]

1. My tree gave me this kind of feeling:
2. Express why your tree was special.

3. Mention some things you feel your tree experienced.

Imagine your tree when it was young, about as young as you are now. When this tree was your age, Indian people lived in this forest. Their clothing, their houses, and their canoes came from trees just like this one. They always said these special words of thanks when they took something from a tree. Read this slowly to yourself: "Look at me, friend. Take pity on us, for there is nothing for which you cannot be used. And it is your way that there is nothing for which we cannot use you. I come to ask for your covering, to make a basket out of you. I pray friend, not to feel angry with me for this. Take care, friend."

Why did the Indians ask the tree not to be angry?

4. Why did they call it "Friend"?

5. List some ways that this tree shows it is a living being.

6. Now consider this: How many things in your home and in your life are made from trees?

7. What would you say to this tree if tomorrow it must be cut down to make something for you?

8. How do you think your tree should be used?

As soon as you finish, sit quietly and wait to be called back by your teacher or leader.[1]

The objective of this lesson is not educational but emotional. The final question on the worksheet summarizes the educators' real lesson objective: "Do you have any different feelings towards trees now than you did before you came here?"

Greenpeace International is promoting its environmental agenda to thousands of schools throughout the country, using its various classroom materials. In one clever scheme it hopes to turn children into environmental activists during Halloween. They suggest that for Halloween children dress as endangered species. A Greenpeace spokesperson "envisions trick-or-treaters lobbying their neighbors to support next year's reauthorization of the Endangered Species Act as they load up on goodies."[2]

Curricula for science lessons are plagued with environmental propaganda. Propagandizing lessons sometimes end with a political action activity suggested in the name of applying the learning. Sometimes the children are urged to write to a government official or the head of a corporation to express their concern on an environmental issue. Teachers are left with the burdensome task of having to decipher between good science and propaganda.

"There's a lot of junk that works itself into the curriculum," admits John Padalino, head of the National Science Teachers Association's task force on environmental education. According to *Education Week*, common errors found in environmental lessons include:

- Condemnation of internal-combustion engines as having worsened the environment. But just in the area of cultivation, the engine has allowed for more efficient farming and contributed to the reforestation of many farmlands.

- School environmental texts routinely scare students with misinformation about "global warming." What is often not taught to children is that atmospheric temperatures are cyclical and that water vapor is a bigger cause of the "greenhouse" effect than is man-produced carbon dioxide.

- Students are often led by environmental propaganda to believe that air quality poses greater risks today than ever before. The fact is, air quality has significantly improved over past decades.

- Some materials still teach students that the aerosol deodorant, hair spray, and paint they use contain chlorofluorocarbons that damage the ozone layer. The fact is, CFCs have not been used in the United States since 1978.[3]

One misleading environmental message routinely drummed into the heads of children is that they can save the planet. While it is fine to be conscientious about consumption and waste, the fact is that in 1987 only 7 percent of the United States' energy usage was attributed to energy consumption in the home. Researcher Eric Miller comments, "In total, the energy used by individuals accounts for only a bit over a quarter of all energy consumption in the nation. This pattern is also true for pollution, for toxic waste, for loss of wetlands, soil erosion, ozone depletion, rain forest destruction, and so forth. . . ."[4]

Still, the hype has paid off for the eco-activists. A survey of college freshman across the country indicated that from 1986 to 1989 the number of students who ranked environmental cleanup as "a very important life goal" jumped from 16 percent to 26 percent. A teen magazine found that readers aged fourteen to twenty-one ranked the environment as the top problem facing America out of a list of twenty choices.[5]

Global Education

An emerging trend in education (and grazing in the same ideological meadow as the eco-educator) is the global educator. Global-education leader Kenneth Tye refers to this trend as a new social movement. He defines a social movement as a "program or set of actions by a significant number of people directed toward a specific social change."[6] Without even questioning whether parents want their children subjected to this change, global educators are rapidly moving to replace traditional studies in Western civilization with courses in global world history, world literature, and global ecology.[7]

Global education is not an add-on course but is a philosophy of education infused throughout the curriculum. It is designed to create "world citizens" out of our youngest (and most naive) American citizens. And it is invariably taught from a liberal political viewpoint. An elementary school in Reading, Massachusetts, for instance, receives supplies from the ultra-liberal Educators for Social Responsibility whom the global educators in that school glowingly describe as "specializing in peace and disarmament issues, including dispelling stereotypes about the USSR."[8]

In Washington state one prominent global-education consortium hosts special speakers to lecture public-school teachers. Speakers have included a Third World feminist economist and a Native American "healer/poet/psychotherapist" who gave a lecture on "the earth as a holistic system."[9] Yet no conservative lecturers were included in the list to offer a different perspective.

Global-education advocate Steven Lamy of the University of Southern California refers to patriotic Americans as "ultraconservatives" and "extremists" because they believe that if there is to be global education its aim should be to "promote U.S. interest and to build domestic and international support for American ideals and traditions."[10]

In his words, these educators are ultraconservative extremists because they "believe in a strong military and a U.S. global strategy that supports intervention when and where American interests are threatened." He claims that these educators are "irresponsibly attempting to deny American students an education that will enable them to compete, cooperate, and live peacefully at home and abroad." He criticizes "the extremists on the right." Why? Because they have the gall to be "supportive of a more traditional educational agenda that focuses on U.S. history, state and local government, U.S. politics, Western civilization, and free-trade economics. They believe that students should be prepared to be American citizens and to represent American interests in a competitive international environment."[11]

To the globalist, teaching American citizens what it means to be American citizens is extremist and irresponsible! What is truly concerning is that Lamy's writings are promoted in a book published by the Association of Supervision and Curriculum Development—an influential 80,000-member organization.

Claiming global peace as their objective the teachers seek to indoctrinate students with a particular vision of how to look at the world. Rather than teaching students how to think they are teaching them what to think. As Kenneth Tye admits, "it calls for a major change in thinking and it has to do with deeply held values."[12]

For instance, the Center for Teaching International Relations, a prominent global education training institute in Denver, suggests an economics lesson for students in which the teacher is to drop dozens of coins on the floor while telling the children to scramble after them. The teacher is then to tell the students to "redistribute" the money "more equitably" among themselves.[13]

"Peace" education is often a component of global education. In a textbook on global education for teacher training one professor writes that the goal of global education is to "be critical of our history of aggression and violence, of the social institutions supporting the values and beliefs contributing to violence."[14]

In global/peace-education programs the United States is the "bad guy." "We have the most violent government on the planet," says liberal writer Colman McCarthy, the founder of the Center for Teaching Peace. He has developed a public-school course on "peace," and hundreds of schools have asked him to help them set up his course.[15]

The problem with "peace" courses is, as was noted earlier by conservative commentator Dennis Praeger, they don't distinguish between good violence and bad violence. Violence ended slavery in America; it ended the Holocaust in Germany; it stopped Saddam Hussein's attempts to grab a major portion of the world's oil supply. Peace courses tend to train students to simply abhor all forms of violence or weapons of war. Again, the emotional education in these courses is more important than the intellectual education.

Students in New Mexico, for example, tried to raise one million dollars to erect a monument in Los Alamos—the birthplace of the atomic bomb—to emphasize peace on the fiftieth anniversary of the bombing of Hiroshima by the United States. Seeing the obvious emotional manipulation of the children by their teachers, Los Alamos city officials agreed to the monument on the condition that it be dedicated on the anniversary of Japan's surrender. After all, that is when peace was achieved during World War II. This "monument to peace" will teach the children little about what is required for peace to occur. But they will spend countless hours *feeling* as if they are truly doing something to promote peace. There couldn't be a better example of a waste of educational time.

Political action is often tied to global education. Students are encouraged to write letters to government officials or raise money for various causes. Steven Lamy points out that "educators who are active in global education programs tend to belong to policy-oriented interest groups (e.g. Sierra Club and Amnesty International). . . . Their interest and spirit of activism far exceed the public norm."[16]

In a junior high school in a suburb of Los Angeles, teachers took their students on a "walk through the real world" in which they visited downtown Los Angeles. These twelve- to fourteen- year-old youngsters were to "study the city and that same evening write recommendations to [the then] Los Angeles Mayor Tom Bradley about how they thought the city should be improved." The teachers who designed this program proudly published a sample of a student's sophomoric work: "Dear Mr. Bradley, you've got problems. Can't you do something to help these people?"[17] But then, what would you expect from a child with little knowledge who is asked to solve complex problems adults wrestle with?

Parents involved in that same school attend a program that takes a "moral look at war." On another night they attend a lecture on the "Fate of the Forest." The purposes of the event were to "educate everyone about the fate of the forests of the world; show students that they can make a difference; and raise funds for the World Wildlife Fund." During International Sports Awareness Day the students play only "noncompetitive games" enjoyed by children in other cultures of the world (sports competition is a nonpeaceful practice).

In global-education schools, students learn a smattering of cultural facts about as many foreign countries as possible. But they learn it at the expense of certain aspects of American culture. Clearly, not enough emphasis is placed on an understanding of American documents such as the Constitution, the Declaration of Independence, or the Mayflower Compact; not enough is being taught about what it means to be an American citizen, both the rights and responsibilities of citizenship. Students don't learn about the Bible and its important contribution to our society, historically and currently. Not enough emphasis is placed on the positive role of capitalism, competition, and freen enterprise and the positive role of American business at home and in the world.

Unfortunately, while students are learning to be "good global citizens," too many of them could not answer questions about American culture with any elaboration. For all their education in multiculturalism, globalism, and peace, students lack a clear understanding of and an appreciation for their American culture. That lack of understanding will hamper their ability to appreciate and benefit from what our culture has to offer. If you don't appreciate something, you don't work to preserve it.

Predictions

1. *Multicultural education will increase in schools as ethnic diversity increases.* Many educators will not make the distinction between ethnicity and culture. Nor will they distinguish the various levels of cultural identity (for instance, the black singer who accepts an award for R&B Artist of the Year and thanks "the Lord" is reflecting both black and Christian cultures). Students in those classes will increasingly define themselves by ethnicity. Ironically, a new form of enthnocentricism may result because of this.

2. *"Peace" education will rise in popularity.* With the demise of the USSR, peace education will focus on domestic issues. These courses will focus mainly on nonviolent conflict resolution with heavy doses of psychology. However, some schools will incorporate moral lessons and emphasize goodness, not just nonviolence.

3. *Global education will flourish in the 1990s.* Consequently, instruction in American culture and citizenship will decline. Being a good American citizen will be equated with being a good world citizen. American history will be taught in the context of world history.

If parents want to counter these liberal trends they will need to take more responsibility for teaching their children the values concerning American citizenship, environmental awareness, and respect for cultural unity. At the same time we must resist the eco- and global educators' aggressive agenda. If we don't, we will lose the America we neglected to preserve and evolve into the America they invented in school.

12
The Gay Nineties:
Homosexuality in the Classroom

I T TRULY WAS an historic evening, the first of its kind. On May 20, 1994, the Los Angeles school district held its first "Gay, Lesbian, and Bisexual Prom" for high school juniors and seniors. A press release from the school district announced that for the first time students "will openly experience the magic that heterosexual students have always taken for granted. They will dance, romance, and dine without fear of exposure or rebuke."[1]

Truly, the Gay Nineties have arrived. The most notable change in sex education today is the increasing acceptance of homosexuality as a normal—even inevitable—lifestyle for students. Throughout the country, school districts are incorporating various aspects of pro-homosexual values. This is a trend that will only increase until, by the early twenty-first century, all school districts will give homosexuals equal respect and consideration alongside heterosexual students. There will be homosexual proms, homosexual youth clubs, homosexual teen support centers, and homosexual sensitivity training for staff and students.

To some this may seem like a ridiculous prediction that will only be true in major urban areas. However, when you look at the rise of the modern homosexual movement in America, the trajectory toward full inclusion begins to make more sense.

The Modern Homosexual Movement

The magnitude of the public's shifting attitude regarding homosexuality is remarkable—from disdain and prosecution to acceptance and promotion. For instance, in 1924 when a man named Henry Gerber founded an organization to promote homosexual rights in Chicago he was quickly arrested, fired from his job, and the organization was shut down. In the 1940s and 1950s, homosexuals were arrested and sentenced to lengthy prison terms for their activity.

However, 1961 marked a quiet shift in the legal standing of homosexuals. In that year the Illinois legislature decriminalized private homosexual activity between consenting adults.[2] By 1986 over half of the states had decriminalized homosexual conduct.

Homosexuals mark June 27, 1969, as the date when the Gay Liberation movement began. On that day patrons of the homosexual bar The Stonewall Inn rioted when New York police raided the establishment. A new era had begun in which gays, lesbians, and bisexuals openly pushed for greater public sympathy and acceptance. Their efforts have paid off.

In 1970 the Institute for Sex Research did a survey that found 49 percent of respondents agreeing with the statement that "homosexuality is a social corruption which can cause the downfall of a civilization." Yet, as quickly as 1977 attitudes had changed. A Harris Poll survey found that by a two-to-one majority Americans favored laws prohibiting job discrimination on the basis of sexual orientation.[3] In 1982 former Vice President Walter Mondale addressed attendees of a gay-rights dinner. The United States Conference of Mayors in 1984 called for the legal protection of homosexuals at all levels of government. That same year, Dr. Virginia Uribe, a lesbian high school teacher in the Los Angeles school district, started a ground-breaking homosexual teen counseling program on campus called Project 10. In less than forty years homosexuals moved from being criminals to being counselors. How could this have happened?

David Greenberg, professor of sociology at New York University, offers several explanations.

1. During the 1960s, "In college, many [students] rebelled against restrictions that appeared to serve no rational purpose and

developed a life-style of moderate hedonism. . . . They sought self-expression and self-realization, rather than conformity to externally imposed behavior standards."[4]

2. "Gender stereotypes were changing fast: in 1967, more than half the freshmen entering college thought that married women should not hold a job, in 1984, less than a quarter agreed." Greenberg comments that "As rigid gender stereotypes weakened, so did resistance to homosexuality."[5]

3. Sex became detached from marriage and was pursued primarily for pleasure. Greenberg writes, "The acceptance of some forms of sexual experience whose sole purpose is pleasure, sociability, or the expression of love makes it hard, in the absence of rational grounds, to reject others that are equally harmless and consensual. Thus there occurred a reduction of hostility toward homosexuality alongside a relaxation of attitudes toward divorce, premarital sex, contraception, abortion, and pornography."[6]

4. Lesbianism became more acceptable because, as feminist Jill Johnston writes, "Lesbianism is the key to liberation and only women who cut their ties to male privilege can be trusted to remain serious in the struggle against male dominance."[7]

5. Greenberg notes that college "social-science courses, which are required for many students, preach cultural relativism. Students are encouraged to question their taken-for-granted values and beliefs. As they go through college they become more liberal and less rejecting of homosexuality."[8]

6. Sociologists began to study homosexuality as a lifestyle rather than narrowly focusing on sexual acts and desires. Greenberg writes that this has a "humanizing effect" on how others see homosexuals. A symbiotic relationship exists between public tolerance of homosexuality and social scientists' work in bringing to light the "normalcy" of the homosexual life. As the public grows more tolerant, sociologists produce more studies that have the effect of encouraging more tolerance.

    7. Academic freedom has protected teachers from those who disagree with their teachings about homosexuality.

When it comes to how public schools teach about homosexuality, two factors seem to dominate the approving—or at least nonjudging—approach taken by teachers. The first is that many educators believe that AIDS education cannot be taught without reference to homosexuality. In the spirit of democratic equality, any reference to homosexuality must, then, be nonjudgmental. In the absence of disapproval, homosexuality is placed on a par with heterosexuality as a form of sexual expression.

In high schools in Lee County, Florida, freshmen (fourteen-year-olds) participate in classroom discussions with AIDS-infected people regarding how to have "safe sex." When they become juniors they can, with parental permission, receive an HIV test at school. The principal of one of the high schools reports that many other schools are inquiring about their AIDS-prevention program. Though Lee County is a pilot for this approach, he predicts that HIV testing will become commonplace in public schools throughout the country.[9] It is unknown what kind of impact "feeling safe" will have on the sexual behavior of students who find they are not infected.

AIDS education has apparently not been effective in convincing gay youth from engaging in high-risk activities. In a city that probably is unequaled in its efforts to educate young people about AIDS, the San Francisco Department of Public Health reports many gay men continue to engage in unprotected sex. Thirty-three percent of young HIV-infected gay men reported having unprotected anal intercourse within the previous six months of the survey.[10]

These alarming findings come nearly ten years after the city began an array of education programs. It can hardly be said that gay men in San Francisco are unaware of AIDS and the need to alter their behavior. School officials should look at such findings before assuming that more explicit AIDS education will significantly alter young people's behavior. Nevertheless, public schools continue to press for more explicit AIDS education programs and include homosexual activity on the acceptable menu of sexual expression for students.

The second major reason homosexuality will increase in its acceptance as a subject in public schools is because educators believe that homosexual teenagers are at great risk of suicide due to the "homophobia" of society at large and the rest of the student population specifically. They then conclude that the only way to reduce the "epidemic" of gay teen suicide is to raise their self-esteem and simultaneously reduce homophobia on campus.

Gay Teen Suicide: Issue or Illusion?

Homosexual advocates have convinced many educators that homosexual youth are committing suicide at alarming rates due to social hostility and self-hate through "internalized homophobia." The Gay and Lesbian Education Commission in Los Angeles, for instance, claims that "Suicide is the leading cause of death for young gays and lesbians. They commit suicide at 3 times the rate of heterosexual youth.[11] They also claim that "Queer youth attempt suicide at 7 times the rate of heterosexual youth."[12]

The state leadership of the Colorado PTA in 1994 tried to pass a resolution "encouraging presentations about homosexuality, bisexuality and transsexuality that include diverse points of view." That state's PTA board defended its actions, claiming that lesbian teenagers were twice as likely to commit suicide as were heterosexual girls, and gay teenagers in general were six times more likely to commit suicide than were their heterosexual classmates. The PTA also claimed that "up to 30 percent of completed youth suicides annually" were done by homosexual youth.[13]

In 1994 Massachusetts enacted a law prohibiting discrimination against gay and lesbian public-school students. One of the reasons lawmakers cited for doing this was that homosexual teenagers attempted suicide at higher rates than heterosexual teens.[14]

In 1989 a Seattle public health educator presented to the Association of Sexuality Education and Training a paper entitled "Why Should the Public Schools Teach about Sexual Orientation?" In it she claimed that "according to the National Institute of Mental Health, they [homosexual students] are 2-3 times as likely to attempt suicide as heterosexual youth."[15]

But is all this handwringing about homosexual teen suicide backed up by research? The answer is no. The extremely inflated numbers bandied about by homosexual advocates are based on only one report published by San Francisco homosexual activist Paul Gibson. His paper, "Gay Male and Lesbian Youth Suicide," was initially included but later dropped from a 1989 government report on youth suicide.[16]

Peter LaBarbera, the editor of *The Lambda Report*, a magazine focusing on the activities of the homosexual rights movement, analyzed Gibson's report and found many serious flaws. For instance, LaBarbera points out that Gibson "refers to one author who speculated in 1985 (in the gay newspaper *The Washington Blade*) that as many as 3,000 gay youths kill themselves a year—a number that exceeds the total number of annual teen suicides by more than a thousand."[17]

LaBarbera points out another research flaw in Gibson's work: "The foundation of Gibson's claim of a soaring rate of gay teen suicides is data culled from surveys at youth assistance or 'drop in' centers. Many of the centers studied are gay-oriented establishments for homeless youth or those facing severe crisis, such as the Institute for the Protection of Gay and Lesbian Youth in New York City. Such sample groups skew the results because they reflect a pool of troubled youth who are naturally more suicidal than a random sample of teens."[18]

Gibson also failed to use a heterosexual control group to put his findings in context. LaBarbera quotes Susan Blumenthal of the National Institute of Mental Health—the organization that rejected Gibson's findings: ". . . [M]any of these studies have a small sample size, lack comparison groups, and have difficulties ascertaining the prevalence of homosexuality in the population being studied."[19]

Gibson claims that gay youth commit suicide because of "internalized homophobia." However, LaBarbara points out that, "Most studies of homosexual suicide attempts find other influencing factors present in their backgrounds that are common to all cases of suicide."[20]

The numbers and percentages that Gibson claims regarding gay youth suicide just don't add up. His findings have been criticized by leading authorities on teen suicide, and they were removed from the government's report on youth suicide. But his report has been used effectively by homosexual advocates to create a sympathetic picture of the "plight" of gay students. In fact, pro-homosexual educational materials still refer to the government's first edition of its "Report on Youth Suicide," which included Gibson's study. For instance, the flawed Gibson study is cited in a brochure advertising a video entitled *Gay Youth* that is marketed to public-school teachers in order to "address the homophobic attitudes and actions often encouraged in the public schools." The brochure claims the video is for "high schools and individuals who care for youth."[21]

Again, victimization is the prevalent theme. Homosexual authors Marshall Kirk and Hunter Madsen define the strategy that is evidenced in so many public schools today:

> In any campaign to win over the public, gays must be portrayed as victims in need of protection so that straights will be inclined by reflex to adopt the role of protector. . . . The purpose of victim imagery is to make straights feel very uncomfortable; that is, to jam with shame the self-righteous pride that would ordinarily accompany and reward their antigay belligerence, and to lay the groundwork for the process of conversion by helping straights identify with gays and sympathize with their underdog status.[22]

Public Schools' Inclusion of Homosexuality

Homosexual "victimization" has been effective in swaying educators. In 1990 the National Education Association passed a resolution urging its local affiliates and member teachers to "support appropriately established sex education programs, including information on . . . diversity of sexual orientation."[23]

In Massachusetts, public-school teachers receive state-sponsored sensitivity training for helping meet the "needs" of gay and lesbian students. A state commission also recommended that schools establish support groups in which homosexual and heterosexual students can meet to discuss gay issues. Furthermore, the commission recommended that gay and lesbian issues be included in all aspects of the curriculum.

In Wisconsin, the state department of education along with other education organizations sponsored a workshop for teachers entitled "A Woman's Place Is in the Curriculum." The only workshop repeated during the three-day conference—presumably to ensure more teachers attended—was "Integrating Lesbian History in the Public School Curriculum."[24]

In 1992 the Los Angeles school district declared June of each year to be "Gay and Lesbian Pride Month." District officials encourage schools to introduce children to homosexual role models, historical figures, and social issues.

In one school a boy was taken from his English class to attend a homosexuality sensitivity session. When the boy's father learned of this he called the principal and other district officials to vehemently protest. The only call the district returned to him was from the district's security office informing him that if he persisted in threatening educators they would have to take action.[25]

In the Seattle area, high schools invite gay and lesbian speakers to address school assemblies during homecoming week as a part of "National Coming Out Day." The homosexuals who promote this hope to legitimize their sexuality in the eyes of the teenagers. Each speaker is accompanied at these assemblies by "other alumni of the same high school, especially politicians, clergy, teachers, law enforcement personnel and others in classic role-model positions."[26]

In a New Hampshire elementary school, the principal invited a gay men's chorus to give a concert to the children. They changed the words of familiar children's songs to sing about boys loving boys and girls loving girls ("Mister Sandman, bring me a dream/ Make him the cutest that I've ever seen"). During their concert they asked the children to raise their hands if they have two mommies or two daddies living with them. One teacher was so embarrassed by the incident, she later told a parent that if the concert hadn't stopped when it did she was going to pull the fire alarm. When challenged by parents, the principal showed no concern that she was ramming her values down the throats of parents. This was part of a multicultural emphasis at the school, but she showed no sensitivity to the Christian, Jewish, and Muslim cultures she trampled on.

The promotion of homosexuality is by no means accepted by all people involved in schools where it occurs. Pro-homosexual programs represent an invasive rather than a natural process within school systems. Controversy often surrounds the inclusion of homosexual curricula, programs, and guest speakers. Still, the movement marches on. While its proponents face hostile reactions from many parents and educators, there is no sign of any abatement of the trend toward full inclusion.

As full inclusion becomes a greater reality, there will be a trend to broaden the definition of sexual "orientation." This will result in more students identifying with homosexual or bisexual orientations. One teachers' glossary on sexual terms, for instance, includes spiritual and emotional attraction in the definition of the term *gender orientation*: "the gender of persons to whom one feels attracted whether one has crushes on, dreams about, falls in love with, or feels romantic/sexual/spiritual/emotional attraction mostly to men, women, or both." It further clarifies that "Whether 'most' people are bisexual depends how it is defined. Most people consider themselves heterosexual; most people also experience some sexual or romantic attraction toward people of their own gender."[27]

In the book *Changing Bodies, Changing Lives*, a sex-education book often used as a resource for teachers, people who are exclusively homosexual or heterosexual are shown as extremes on a spectrum. Most people, the authors assert, are somewhere in between with tendencies toward one direction.

One public health educator justifies the inclusion of homosexual programs in schools by manufacturing the notion that classrooms are packed with students who are homosexuals or who have homosexuals in their immediate family. Here's how she concludes that as many as nine students in every classroom are in this situation:

> Various researchers and social scientists report that 4-10 percent of Americans consider themselves gay or lesbian. That means a high school student body of 1,000 has between 40 and 100 gay or lesbian students (and that doesn't count bisexual youth). If students have, on average, 1.5 siblings, then approximately 60 to 150 have a gay brother or a lesbian sister.

If even 1-2 percent of parents are gay, then an additional 20 to 40 students have a gay dad or a lesbian mom. That means that 1 to 3 out of every 10 students either is gay him or herself, or has an immediate family member who is. That's between 3 and 9 kids in every class of 30![28]

While all educators do not believe that kind of stratospheric projections, such claims are impacting school policies and teacher training. For instance, the Institute for Sexual Inclusiveness through Training and Education (INSITE) makes nine recommendations for public schools. It includes: "Change heterosexist language," "Conduct in-service 'sensitivity' training for administrators and all school personnel," "Provide 'sensitivity' training for students," "Introduce gay/lesbian issues into all curriculum areas," and "Provide supportive settings for sexual minority youth."[29]

For teachers INSITE recommends the following:

- "Change language that assumes everyone is or should be heterosexual (use 'partner' rather than girl/boyfriend, 'permanent relationship' rather than marriage)."

- "Identify gay/lesbian contributions throughout the curriculum (history, literature, art, science, religion, etc.)."

- "Provide history of oppression (such as Holocaust, origin of the word 'faggot')."

- "Submit requests to improve library holdings (both fiction and nonfiction) related to sexual diversity."

- "Develop and/or advertise resources (support groups) for lesbian/gay students and their families."

- "Include issues for gay/lesbian students and staff in coverage in school newspaper."

- "Bring in openly lesbian/gay adults as resources in classes and assemblies."

- "Include gay/lesbian concerns in all prevention programs (suicide, dropout, pregnancy, etc.) and in training of peer leaders, student government, etc."[30]

Those who oppose the inclusion of homosexual subjects in schools are often labeled "homophobic" or "heterosexist." *Homophobia* is an especially nonsensical term since it is most often used to describe anyone who even disagrees with the pro-homosexual agenda. Everyone who dissents from the homosexual agenda is said to have a phobia. In that case Republicans could be labeled "Demophobic," Democrats could be labeled "Republiphobic," and anyone who disagrees with anyone else could be accused of having a phobia.

However, in some circles, homophobia and heterosexism take on even more absurd meanings. The United Way of the Bay Area Task Force on Lesbian and Gay Issues provides us with a list of various indications of someone who is plagued with homophobia or heterosexism:

- "Looking at a lesbian or gay person and automatically thinking of their sexuality rather than seeing them as whole, complete persons." [Even though sexuality is the defining issue for homosexuals.]

- "Failing to be supportive when your gay/lesbian friend is sad about a quarrel or breakup." [Even though you do have the homosexual as a friend in the first place, that is not enough.]

- "Not asking about your gay/lesbian friend's lover, although you regularly ask, 'How is your husband or wife?' when you run into a heterosexual friend." [Again, the fact that you have a homosexual friend is not enough.]

- "Wondering which one is the 'man'/'woman' in a lesbian/gay couple." [Idle curiosity is indication of a phobia or prejudice?]

- "Feeling that lesbian/gay people are too outspoken about gay rights." [They can never be too outspoken?]

- "Being outspoken about lesbian/gay rights but making sure everyone knows that you are straight."[31] [Even being a supporter of homosexual rights is not enough!]

Total indifference to sexual orientation is one goal of homosexual advocates with promotion of the lifestyle being another. Once homosexuality has been fully included in education and the majority of students are stripped of any bias against homosexual conduct, once the sexually ambivalent child is told that homosexuality is not only an acceptable option but quite possibly inevitable, once students are given homosexual support groups and put in contact with adult homosexual groups, then school officials will have a new problem to deal with (though by then many may not see it as a problem): adult-child sexual activity *initiated by the child.*

13
Pedophilia: The Next Civil Right?

T HE THOUGHT THAT adult-child sexual relations could one day be legitimized by schools and society seems so absurd and alarmist I hesitate to write about its possibility with any certainty. However, forecasting social trends requires that we look not merely at the climate of society now but at the slow movement of social patterns over long periods of time. We must examine the glacier-like creeping of social behavior and beliefs. And we must look at what trendsetters are saying regarding a particular issue.

With this in mind, acceptance of adult-child sexual relations—pedophilia—becomes a very real possibility, though it is hard to imagine this occurring for at least thirty or forty years (similarly to the rapid acceptance of homosexuality). Lester Kirkendall, founding board member of the Sex Information and Education Council of the United States (SIECUS), one of the most influential sex-education organizations in America, wrote in a 1985 article entitled "Sex Education in the Future" that one day sex-education courses "will probe sexual expression . . . with same-sex [partners]" and "even across . . . generational lines." He observed that with "a diminished sense of guilt . . . these patterns will become legitimate" and "the emphasis on normality and abnormality will be much diminished with future trends."[1]

Man/boy love—as pedophiles refer to it—has historically been a part of the larger homosexual movement. The homosexual community is divided over whether pedophilia should be a part of their push for sexual liberation. It appears, however, that much of the resistance to pedophilia within the homosexual community has to do with its desire for greater acceptance by society.

David Thorstad, former president of New York's Gay Activists Alliance and founding member of the North American Man/Boy Love Association, writes that "although man/boy love represented a minority phenomenon within the gay subculture, it was far from unusual."[2] Thorstad points to ten years of research done by Alan Bell and Martin Weinberg, who found that 25 percent of white gay men and 14 percent of black gay men had had sex with boys sixteen years old or younger when they themselves were twenty-one or older.[3]

While homosexuals point to June of 1969 as the start of the gay rights movement, pedophiles within the homosexual movement point to December of 1977 as their point of organization. They organized in response to the arrest of twenty-four men in Revere, Massachusetts, for having sex with underage boys. The following year the first activist organization for pedophiles formed under the name The North American Man/Boy Love Association (NAMBLA). Their goal: to push for the repeal of age-of-consent laws.

In 1979 a national conference on homosexual rights adopted a resolution urging "full rights for gay youth, including revision of the age of consent laws."[4] But due to a strong reaction from lesbians within the conference, a compromise resolution was later passed that called for the protection of "lesbian and gay youth from any laws which are used to discriminate against, oppress, and/or harass them in their homes, schools, jobs and social environment."[5] The difference was semantic.

NAMBLA participated in the 1984 Lesbian/Gay Freedom Day Parade although some homosexuals opposed their inclusion. In 1985 NAMBLA was admitted to New York's Council of Lesbian and Gay Organizations by a close vote.

While the man/boy love movement has made strides toward greater acceptance, it has also had opposition. In 1983 for instance, Wisconsin decriminalized homosexual acts but made sex between an adult and a sixteen-year-old a felony. Also, the majority of sex research and social workers still see adult/child sex as inherently abusive.

However, there are prominent sex-education leaders who quietly support the expansion of sexual rights to include noncoercive pedophilia. John DeCecco, the head of the human sexuality program at San Francisco State University, comments, "I argue more on the side of liberty and keeping doors open and options open." He goes on to say, "The decision should largely rest in the hands of the people who are entering into the relationship. If I'm 12 and I decide to have sex with a 19-year-old or a 20-year-old or a 50-year-old, that is really a choice I have."[6]

Wardell Pomeroy, a SIECUS founding board member and the author of Boys and Sex and Girls and Sex, told *Time* magazine that incest, "can sometimes be beneficial" to children.[7] He later explained, "People seem to think that any contact between children and adults . . . has a bad effect on the child. I say that this can be a loving and thoughtful, responsible sexual activity."[8]

While SIECUS officially opposes adult-child sexual contact, Mary Calderone, the co-founder and past president of the organization, is soft on the issue. She said in an interview, "It's not that it's a bad thing or a wicked thing, it just simply should not be part of life in general, right out on the sidewalk."[9]

Dr. John Money is Professor Emeritus of Medical Psychology and Pediatrics at Johns Hopkins University. In an interview in *Paidika*, a magazine promoting pedophiles' rights that is published in the Netherlands, he stated: "[I]f I were to see the case of a boy aged ten or eleven who's intensely erotically attracted toward a man in his twenties or thirties, if the relationship is totally mutual, and the bonding is genuinely totally mutual, then I would not call it pathological in any way."[10]

Dr. Money, an influential force in sex research, stated, "I have absolutely no doubt that the vast majority of paedophiles [European spelling] who are put in jail have no business being in jail at all."[11]

Harvard Health Services psychologist Douglas Powell comments, "I have not seen anyone harmed by this so long as it occurs in a relationship with somebody who really cares about the child."[12]

Family therapist Larry Constantine thinks that children "should have the right to express themselves sexually, which means that they may or may not have contact with people older than themselves."[13]

Dr. Gerald Jones, formerly a research scholar at the University of Southern California, writes that research has found "benign or even beneficial results in boys who were at the time involved with men and in adults who had been involved in sexual relationships with adult men when they were boys."[14]

The editorial board of *Paidika* includes Dr. Vern Bullough, dean of faculty of natural and social science at State University College at Buffalo, New York; Dr. Wayne Dynes of Hunter College; Dr. John DeCecco from the department of psychology at San Francisco State University; and Dr. Hurbert Kennedy, a research associate at the Center for Research and Education in Sexuality at San Francisco State University. Under *Paidika's* "Statement of Purpose" the editors write,

> The starting point of Paidika is necessarily our consciousness of ourselves as paedophiles. . . . We shall be speaking, therefore, not only to paedophiles seeking a greater understanding of their identity, but also to members of the academic community open to objective investigation of the phenomenon. . . . [W]e intend to demonstrate that paedophilia has been, and remains, a legitimate and productive part of the totality of human experience.[15]

Strategies for Inclusion

Acceptance of pedophilia will most likely take a few decades, though the basis for it, founded on current thinking about sexuality, is already firmly in place. The existing attitudes toward sex education and homosexual youth have created a rationale for adult/child sex. The only hindrance to full inclusion is emotional rather than rational arguments (society at large has long ago abandoned the moral arguments regarding sexuality). When we study the writings of pro-pedophile literature we begin to see a strategy for inclusion emerging.

1. *Universalization.* Sex researchers will assert that adult/child sex has been around since the dawn of time and in every corner of the earth. Pedophile advocates will assert that historical examples in Greece and Europe as well as bisexual relations in primitive cultures point to the universality of adult/child sex. They will make the argument that since pedophiles have been and continue to be a part of every society pedophilia cannot be viewed as abnormal.

2. *Naturalization.* Sex researchers will assert that pedophilia is natural. Dr. John Money, for instance, suggests that pedophilia is "an orientation which cannot be changed or permanently suppressed."[16] Three pedophile advocates wrote in the *Journal of Homosexuality,* "The pedophile identity formation is viewed parallel to the homosexual's" in how the person comes to see himself.[17] A senior clinical psychologist at a hospital in Scotland writes sympathetically that pedophiles "feel their sexual desire for children is a natural part of their constitution."[18]

As sex education becomes more explicit at earlier grades could it have the effect of giving children more sexual options? In the name of preparing children for unwanted sexual contact by adults, could it be possible that it is also empowering the seemingly "sophisticated" child to choose to accept such contact and possibly even initiate it? One sociologist and pedophile supporter writes that "many adult pedophiles say that boys actively seek out sex partners."[19]

Pedophile advocates will invert the issue of civil rights. Rather than talk of adults' rights to have sex with children, they will argue that children should have the right to have sex with whomever they want—including adults.

As we discussed in the last chapter, schools are rapidly moving toward the acceptance of homosexual youth—even homosexual children—as natural and inevitable. With this kind of sex-education framework, school officials cannot rationally argue that gay youth should only have sex with other gay youth. Moral and rational barriers having been removed, the only barrier to man-boy sex is age-of-consent laws. And that is exactly where pedophile advocates will focus their attention. Dr. John Money, responding to an interviewer's question of whether he advocates attacking age-of-consent laws to advance pedophilia, said, "I certainly think that's where we have to begin."[20] While there is greater interest in investigating adult-child sex, scientific research does not have to be available for pedophile advocates to seek social change. Dr. Money continues:

> When the gay rights activists began being politically active, there wasn't a sufficient body of scientific information for them to base their gay rights activism on. So, you don't have to have a basic body of scientific information in order to decide to work actively for a particular ideology. As long as you're prepared to be put in jail. Isn't that how social change has always taken place, really?[21]

3. *Normalization.* If pedophilia is universal and natural, then, it will be argued, it is normal. Pedophile advocates assert that the real reason pedophiles have emotional problems is that society does not accept them:

> On a theoretical level, pedophilia has become an exclusive sexual orientation, classified as one of the sexual disorders. This assumption dominates the diagnosis and the treatment of pedophiles. We don't exclude the possibility that in some cases pedophile practices result from a pathological development, as, in fact, can happen in all sexual orientations. However, we believe that a lot of the problems people with pedophile desires are confronted with result from societal rejection.[22]

The logical destination of the current philosophy of sexual relativism, in which a great variety of pleasure-seeking activities are tolerated, is the tolerance of pedophilia. Interviewing pedophiles, a researcher found they defended their actions based upon the idea that "there can be no absolute standard; normality is relative, so pedophilia cannot be a priori deemed abnormal."[23]

It would not take much for society to accept pedophilia. First, various psychiatric associations would label it an orientation rather than a disorder. Second, states would begin lowering the age of consent to twelve or thirteen. Third, talk shows would begin featuring young teens who appear normal and well adjusted and have sex with a "special adult" in their lives. At first viewers would be shocked, but eventually they would shake their heads and say "live and let live."

While it still seems inconceivable that this could happen, we only need to ask if it would have been conceivable thirty years ago that by the late 1980s openly homosexual teachers would be counseling students about sexual alternatives, that homosexuals would be invited into classes as guest speakers, and that schools would sponsor homosexual support groups and "get-acquainted" dances for students.

In 1993 a Bronx High School teacher named Peter Melzer was removed from his position and placed in a nonteaching role because of his membership in NAMBLA and because he was acting as editor of a pedophile newsletter. School officials rightly cited New York's law regarding dismissal for immoral conduct. What is disturbing is the response of some students, parents, teachers, and "civil liberties" advocates who wanted him retained since they felt he posed no threat to students. The director of Forensic Mental Health Associates defended the pedophile, stating that if "there is no evidence that he is a predator and he would take advantage of children under his care, he should retain his position as a teacher."[24] So goes the start of cultural change.

The Value of Learning in the Orphanage

ADELE JONES WAS a no-nonsense algebra teacher in Georgetown, Delaware. She got fired for it. School principal John McCarthy said she was guilty of giving "negative grades" and damaging her students' self-esteem—apparently a dismissible offense in his school.[1]

Jones's colleagues, however, considered her a good teacher. "One of the hardest-working teachers in the building," said one. She routinely started the day at 7:15 A.M. and stayed until 6:00 P.M. tutoring struggling students after school. If students didn't work hard—didn't take notes, didn't do their homework, and didn't study for tests—they didn't pass.

That was too much for the principal. "I have made it very clear that one of my goals is to decrease the failure rate, to make sure that kids feel good about learning, stay in class, stay in school, and do well," he testified at the school-board hearing on the matter. He testified that students should "feel good about instruction, feel good about teaching and learning." In talking to a reporter, he drew on his own experience as a former music teacher and band director to criticize the math teacher. When he was a music teacher, he explained, he didn't expect his students to finish the year as musicians. He just wanted them to know more about music than when they started. Such reasoning from a man who is working on his doctorate on "student outcomes."[2]

An English teacher in New York City complained of the same pressure from administrators to pass students who deserve to fail. She wrote:

> The superintendent of our district projected a goal to improve the passing statistics in his district; he naturally apprised our principal of this concern, who in turn reproached our departmental supervisor that some teachers in his department had generated unacceptable passing statistics last term. . . . Certainly those of us who adhere to our requirements are being harassed; there is no other way to describe such administrative heavy-handedness.[3]

Commentator Alston Chase calls this the "learning-is-fun and nobody-should-fail" philosophy and blames it for a loss of the American work ethic among teenagers. "You can see it in the body language of students at any American high school—slumped at their desks as though their spines are made of pasta."[4]

At least one study indicates that a major difference between American education and education in other countries is the attitude toward learning. Researchers at Western Carolina University found that Americans tend to want learning to be fun while parents, teachers, and students of countries with more successful schools view education as serious business. The study found that in Japan when students are sick, it is not uncommon for their mothers to attend class and take notes for them. American students spend more time watching television and less time doing homework. They also found that, contrary to popular myth, more rigorous academic studies in foreign countries did not lead to higher rates of suicide than those in the United States.[5] Hard work won't kill American students.

This gets to the crux of the matter. Any reform is only as good as the teachers and students who must use it every day. Policymakers and think-tank specialists can develop beautiful systems for elaborate reforms. On paper the plans are inspiring. But what counts most is the teacher who gets in front of the class each morning and the student who sits in the desk. If the combined attitude of both teacher and student (and by extension—parent) does not reinforce excellence every day, progress will be lost. Every day is a push upstream against ignorance and incompetence. Both teacher and learner can never cease to vigorously row against the current or both will move backward.

Put another way, information, technology, and needed skills rapidly change in our society. Students who stand still will watch the tail lights of opportunity pass them by, and they will be left in the dust.

To be sure, the vast majority of teachers want their students to achieve well, and they work hard to that end. But somewhere along the line too many teachers' good intentions don't translate into higher-achieving students.

In science, seventeen-year-olds' achievement was lower in 1992 than in 1970, according to statistics from the U. S. Department of Education. However, the good news is that after a sharp decline in the early 1980s achievement has made progress.[6]

There has been no increase in the percentage of high-schoolers functioning at the highest level of science proficiency. (Only 9 percent of these students achieved the highest level of science proficiency in 1990—the same percentage as in 1977.) But there has been some increase in the number of students who can operate at the second highest level. Only four out of ten (42 percent) of seventeen-year-olds operated at this level in 1977, and almost five out of ten (47 percent) could do so in 1992.[7]

In math, all seventeen-year-olds tested in 1992 demonstrated a knowledge of "some basic addition and subtraction facts." However, only 59 percent were categorized as being able to "compute with decimals, simple fractions, and commonly encountered percents." Representing no change from 1978, only 7 percent of seventeen-year-olds operated at the most advanced level—able to solve multistep problems, use basic geometry, work with square roots, and solve problems using algebra.[8]

Reading is an essential skill for success in virtually any job, and it is important in maintaining a well-informed and well-reasoned democracy. It is disturbing then that only 7 percent of seventeen-year-olds are proficient at reading specialized and challenging information—the type of thing they would encounter in a college textbook. There was some improvement of seventeen-year-olds at the midlevel reading ability.[9]

Writing skills are also important for educational progress and success in careers. Not only is writing important as a means of communication, it is also important for developing precise and articulate habits of thinking. It is alarming then that American students cannot write well. On a scale from 100 (unsatisfactory) to 400 (elaborated), eleventh-graders scored only 212 points (just barely above a "minimal" level of 200). Even more alarming is that these high school students performed only 29 points better than fourth-graders. Put another way, children in fourth grade wrote at 17 points below minimal levels and teenagers in eleventh grade wrote at only 12 points above minimal levels. "Minimal" is defined as able to recognize the elements needed to complete the task but unable to use them well enough to ensure a satisfactory answer. The average high school student was nowhere near the 300 level of "adequate," and only in their dreams could these students have achieved level 400 or "elaborated" with the poorly developed skills they had.[10]

The most gains in the past two decades have been made by black students. Hispanics were at the same level in 1990 as they were in 1977 in science but have made impressive gains in reading and writing and some gains in mathematics.[11]

Reform-Weary Teachers

However, for all the effort at reform in the past, many educators are skeptical of new reforms. Merle Marsh, the academic dean of a school in Maryland, writes that when someone mentions reform, "We yawn, and say, 'Is it team teaching again or core curriculum or open space?'"[12]

Veteran teacher James Steffensen, who has been involved with education reform efforts since President Eisenhower, writes:

> For nearly a half century I have watched and participated as one school reform effort after another soared briefly over the horizon and then fell back to earth as awkwardly as a wounded sea gull. Little residue remains of those endeavors except that deposited upon the innovators and designers who conceived and profited from the idea. . . . "What will the public schools of America in the year 2000 look like?" With the exception of the few "innovative" programs which

network television dutifully covers each fall as school opens, the outlook is bleak. There is no reason to believe they will be any more responsive to the education needs of individual children or to national crises than they are today.[13]

Douglas Carnine, a professor of education at the University of Oregon, writes, "Veteran teachers find themselves labeled 'afraid of change' and 'burned out' when they recognize some of today's reforms to be re-labeled experiments that have already failed in the past."[14]

In fact, on some national education commissions, outstanding classroom teachers are largely ignored. One member of such a committee complained that when he joined a top-level commission concerning Chapter 1, "I suggested that it include several outstanding teachers and principals. The response? 'Not necessary.' The commission included three lawyers, and its leadership hired two more. But they would not include a current teacher or principal." Later this committee member "urged that the commission hold hearings with teachers, administrators, and parents around the country before beginning to develop, or to finalize, its recommendations. The response, again, was 'no.' We urged that the commission visit outstanding Chapter 1 schools to talk directly with those who are actually making a difference in the lives of youngsters. 'Not necessary.'"[15]

A survey of teachers found that 76 percent believed that school reforms had not benefited the students who need help the most. Only 9 percent of teachers surveyed said they believe schools use solid research to decide the effectiveness of a new teaching approach. Carnine concluded:

> Educators at all levels, from classroom teachers to national policymakers, routinely use and approve materials and techniques without testing or evaluating them. . . . [I]n education, untested fads sweep through the profession, gathering authority by the number of schools using them, not by proven gains in learning. The field does not distinguish between innovations which merely create change, and reforms which are changes that yield improvements in student achievement.[16]

An example of pushing teachers into dubious "reforms" is California's new approach to teaching math. Even though education leaders admit that anywhere between 50 to 90 percent of teachers are not equipped to teach the new approach, the state insists on moving ahead. Maureen DiMarco, Governor Pete Wilson's top education adviser, is a strong critic of the new math and says there is no research to show that students will do better with the new approach. The state may have to spend $500 million to retrain teachers over the next several years, but they will start the program before the teachers are trained. School districts through-out the state will spend around $250 million just on new textbooks to get on board with the latest fad in math.[17]

Watered Down Academics

Students are taking more academic courses than they have for the past sixty years. Student enrollment in courses such as English, mathematics, science, foreign languages, and social studies went from 67 percent in the late 1920s to as low as 57 percent in 1961. Academic enrollment figures began to increase that year and reached 66 percent in 1990. At the same time nonacademic courses such as home economics, physical education, health, and music increased from 33 percent to a 43 percent peak in 1961. By 1990 it had decreased to 34 percent.[18] Good news!

However, the researchers at the University of Michigan who did the study caution that, "Many of the academic courses [students] are taking are academic in name only."[19] A course may be called "English" but it may not have a rigorous curriculum of grammar and composition or a challenging reading of literature. Courses such as "consumer math" are labeled academic but can be taught without real mathematical studies.

In many instances teachers are explicitly or implicitly pressured by administrators to make their courses easier or to inflate their students' grades. Sometimes schools do this thinking they are helping students' self-esteem; other times administrators do this to make their schools look better.

In 1994, a survey of 237,777 college freshmen revealed that 27 percent reported their grade point averages were A-minus or better. It makes you want to say "Hurrah!" for these students—until you realize that in 1969 only 12.5 percent did that well. Considering that students today have not made much progress over their 1969 counterparts on standardized tests, the only viable explanation seems to be grade inflation by teachers. The survey found that more than 84 percent of college freshmen reported receiving a grade point average of B-minus or better. The traditional bell curve with most students receiving C grades has transformed into a wave cresting toward the inflated A's.[20]

Hard Work and High Skills

Research in thinking skills has found that one thing that separates experts in a field from less-than-expert practitioners is that experts are so skilled at the basics they can quickly move to more advanced and creative problem solving. Many of today's students have not mastered basic academic skills and are thus handicapped in reaching skills levels necessary for real success in our high-technology society. If, for instance, a student does not read with a high level of proficiency, he or she will focus a majority of his or her energy on simply trying to decipher the meaning of a text. He will have little mental energy left to elaborate on how to apply the text's information or how it correlates with other information outside the text. It's like the beginner snow-skier who is struggling so hard just to get down the mountain he can't enjoy the subtle beauties along the way. All he knows is that he is cold and tired and must put all his concentration into making the next turn. For all the talk of "higher-order thinking skills," too many students don't have enough of a grasp on lower order skills to adequately function on a higher level.

Until we come to terms with the appropriate balance between fun and work, leisure and discipline, the latest slew of "top-down" reforms will be foiled by the attitudes of students, parents, and teachers.

Outcome-Based Education

Outcome-based education is the most recent attempt by public schools to achieve better academic results. It represents a radically new approach to the process of education. Let's spend some time looking at it since it is such a hotly debated issue in many school districts. Outcome-based education (OBE) advocates point out that, traditionally, education has focused on inputs rather than outcomes; policymakers, according to OBE proponents, paid more attention to how many hours students sat in math class than how well students actually learned something. While these inputs remained fixed, the outcomes—skills and knowledge— varied greatly among students. OBE attempts to reverse the relationship between what is fixed and what is variable. It wants to structure school around fixed learning outcomes and create flexible time and means for reaching those outcomes.

William Spady, a leading OBE advocate, writes that in the traditional school, "When and how students learn something is more important than what and whether students learn well." In an OBE school, he writes, "What and whether students learn well is more important than when and how they learn it."[21]

It will undoubtedly come as a surprise to many parents that traditional schools have not focused primarily on whether students learn well. Spady has highlighted a major problem with many schools: They have become student-producing factories. As the child moves down the assembly line each factory worker attempts to install a component. However, the child keeps moving down the line whether or not the component is properly installed. At the end of the twelve-year conveyor belt, students are sorted by the quality-control standards of colleges and employers who select from the pile of students the schools churn out each year. Of course, in schools where this misguided thinking does occur it is no wonder the students have mediocre achievement.

However, OBE advocates have not made a sufficient case that problems today in education are due to traditional time-based approaches. Conservatives have long believed that the problem in education is primarily one of poor execution. Nothing in the OBE literature is convincing that execution by teachers will improve under the new structure of OBE.

Spady lists four vital principles of proper OBE execution: (1) clarity of focus on what students are to learn, (2) expanded opportunity and support for successful learning, (3) high expectations, and (4) designing backward from final outcomes to daily lessons.[22] As important as these principles are, they are not unique to OBE. Good teachers in traditional schools use them. Any good teacher must clearly define the learning objective, provide lots of support and opportunities to reach the objective, maintain high expectations, and develop effective lesson plans that relate to the primary learning objective.

Poor Execution

Low student motivation due to having many opportunities to complete an assignment or pass a test is an example of poor execution of the OBE principle of "expanded opportunity." The idea is that students should have opportunities to improve their assignments since the process of refining their homework helps them learn. Many parents complain that this approach to homework demotivates their children, who figure they don't need to work hard on first drafts. Spady laments this problem and reminds educators that expanded opportunities cannot be divorced from high expectations.[23] Still, execution of the lesson plan is inevitably the problem.

Teachers who are currently ineffective and inefficient in lesson planning and execution certainly would benefit from training in these four principles, but it does not require the massive restructuring of OBE to have teachers implement them.

While it is refreshing that many schools are focusing more precisely on the results of their efforts it is disturbing that this has not been their focus all along. Unwittingly, educators who cheer OBE are condemning their own past performance. What are they saying about themselves when they admit that for the past several decades they have not primarily focused on the quality of student learning? When OBE advocates denounce the old system in favor of the new they are denouncing their own ability to produce quality. Why should the public entrust these same educators with being quality-control inspectors in the new system? Spady comments that "OBE implementers have to address the issue of trust by parents," and he offers the suggestion that parents should trust teachers who at least admit they have had past problems.[24]

OBE also suffers from an inherent contradiction. Advocates assert that they can replace the bell curve of achievement with a standard bar of outcome standards. Rather than have time be the inflexible feature of education and achievement be variable, they hope to make results fixed and allow flexibility in how long a student can take to learn the content or master the skill. Time is on the students' side in lower grades where a student has many years of education still ahead. However, as graduation day approaches for the high school senior, the element of time becomes rigid.

The question that OBE advocates must grapple with is how they will handle this inevitable march of time which they claim so oppresses the current system. There are only so many days in a school year and only so many years a student can attend school. Under the current system educators give students one quarter or one semester to learn a certain amount of information. Under the OBE system this time frame is eliminated and a focus on subject mastery allows for greater time to learn the information and skill. However, as graduation day approaches, all students will not meet all the same outcomes simultaneously. Two assumptions of OBE seem at odds: (1) Students learn at different paces and need greater time to achieve a fixed set of outcomes; (2) All students will demonstrate a fixed set of outcomes by the spring of their senior year.

"OBE doesn't guarantee that all kids will graduate at the same level. But it will teach all the fundamentals by graduation," says Spady.[25] To address the time-versus-achievement dilemma, OBE proponents advocate one of two graduation scenarios: (1) Students may graduate at any age as long as they have met the required outcomes; high schools could be filled with students well into their twenties. (2) A school would maintain a specific graduation day but would issue different types of diplomas or use the students' transcripts as a performance diploma. Any college or employer could then see a student's true performance in any given subject.

In the end, OBE cannot escape the bell curve of achievement. It either sets up a bell curve of age, or it leaves the job of sorting by achievement to colleges and employers. If the bell curve is inevitable, OBE still may be valid if it raises academic standards and achievement. However, many within public education question whether it will.

The Association of Supervision and Curriculum Development, an influential organization in education, raises serious questions about OBE schools:

If some common outcomes will be held for all students, will they represent more than minimum competency? To what extent should outcomes stress traditional academic content versus more global skills and proficiencies? How will schools deal with the logistics of educating students who learn at different rates or through different learning styles? According to both supporters and opponents, OBE advocates have failed to answer these questions well enough to win widespread public support for OBE.[26]

Controversial Outcomes

Besides the structural problem of effectively implementing outcome-based education, there are many problems with deciding what the outcomes should be. One positive result of OBE is that the public is able to clearly see what educators expect of students. On issues concerning values this has been particularly eye-opening for many parents.

For instance, Kansas's "outcome number 8" states, "Students have the physical and emotional well-being necessary to live, learn, and work in a global society." To assess more specifically if this outcome has been reached each school district must develop performance indictors. The Kansas Department of Education suggests that students demonstrate achievement of outcome number 8 by being able to, among other things:

- "Explain and demonstrate on a model how to perform breast and testicular self-examination."
- "Explain and demonstrate on a model proper application of a condom."
- "Demonstrate parenting and child care skills."
- "Demonstrate ability to effectively deal with family anger."
- "Express comfort with sexual identity."
- "Express pleasure when participating in movement and physical activity."
- "Limit intake of sugar, fat, and salt."

- "Limit intake of high-calorie foods."
- "Use birth control to prevent unwanted pregnancy each time sexual activity occurs."

Two very serious problems arise from these criteria for student performance: (1) What is acceptable? For instance, what is an acceptable limit on the intake of high-calorie foods? (2) How do educators measure the performance? How is a teacher supposed to measure the level of pleasure a student expresses when "participating in movement and physical activity"? Furthermore, what does expressing pleasure have to do with demonstrating skills in PE class?

OBE did not create the controversial lesson objectives; it forced educators to clearly articulate them. OBE is a structure for education. It has caused educators to bring into the open many of their formerly unspoken nonacademic pap.

Albert Shanker, president of the American Federation of Teachers, criticizes OBE standards as largely nonacademic. "OBE reformers have the rhetoric of higher standards down pat," says Shanker. "They talk about world-class standards and the skills needed to compete in a global economy. But whereas the education standards in other industrialized countries call for things like solving algebraically and by graph simultaneous linear equations or analyzing the causes for the Cold War, OBE standards are vague and fluffy."[27]

As proof, he highlighted Pennsylvania's education outcomes, which included, "All students know and use, when appropriate, community health resources," and an Ohio educator's idea of a graduation outcome being that students "function as a responsible family member." Even academic outcomes are frustratingly vague. Pennsylvania, for instance, wanted students to "write for a variety of purposes, including to narrate, inform, and persuade, in all subject areas." Shanker rightly points out, "In an excellent school, this could mean a portfolio of short stories, several 1,000-word essays and numerous shorter ones. In a poor school, it could mean three short paragraphs loaded with misspellings." In a stunning observation (for Shanker), he comments that the religious right is "correctly suspicious of the outcomes proposed by outcomes-based education."[28]

Dictating Outcomes

Not only are conservative parents outraged by the content of many outcomes, they are suspicious of the process school districts use to develop local outcomes. It is curiously coincidental that while outcome-based education is supposed to include parents and community members in defining the local outcomes, school districts across the country are similar if not identical in their "community-formulated" outcomes.

Many parents report feeling "hustled" or "pushed aside" by their local district after the district invited them to help formulate outcomes. Typically, parents are invited to come to a meeting in which they are divided into smaller groups led by a facilitator from the school district. Each group is asked to brainstorm a list of outcomes they want the schools to adopt. All the lists are then displayed on overheads or on large sheets of butcher paper. However, when the district issues its "community-developed" list of outcomes, the list looks almost identical to lists from other districts, and many of the parent-generated outcomes are absent. For instance, one parent wrote:

> The appointed "Strategic Planning Committee" which developed the Strategic Plan in my home town changed or threw out more than two dozen goals that were supported 100 percent by the local "action teams" that developed them. Despite all the pandering about "local control" which invariably accompanies talk about strategic planning, the outcome of the planning is unquestionably preordained. . . . The action team I participated in had recommended that "legible handwriting" should be a goal for all children by the time they graduate from high school. The Strategic Planning Committee threw it out without discussion. Later, I was told that the goal was inappropriate because it would discriminate against people who couldn't write legibly.[29]

Another parent in a different state reported that "the teachers worked in in-service training from the school district on OBE for three years before coming to parents with the particulars. During that time we were encouraged to help the district form a mission statement. We met in groups with a mix of teachers and parents. I felt manipulated by the teachers to use their terminology. The end result was a mission statement that sounded more like the district wrote it than the parents."[30]

Another parent who spoke out against the heavy-handedness of her district and the direction its restructuring was headed was warned by a school staff member not to buck the system since her twelfth-grade daughter was up for a scholarship.[31]

School officials want parental support but are not serious about parental control. Many district administrators aren't even serious about teachers controlling educational objectives. In a recent survey of fifty-three thousand teachers, only 37 percent believed they had much influence over establishing curriculum at the district level. Even when referring to their own classroom, only 60 percent felt they had considerable control over the content, topics, and skills they taught.[32] The official pronouncements of "community consensus" in reality ring hollow. Furthermore, even when school districts list academically oriented outcomes in social studies, science, math, and foreign language, the actual classroom activities to achieve those outcomes can be questionable.

For instance, in the early 1990s Iowa's guide to teaching math suggested the following guilt-inducing activity: "Calculate energy consumption of the electrical appliances which a U.S. family would normally use on a winter evening. Calculate the amount of fossil fuel used to produce this electricity. Calculate how much energy would have to be produced if every person in China used the same amount of energy as does the typical American."[33] Nowhere does the manual suggest that students calculate the benefits of energy consumption in America—how many jobs are produced, how many lives are saved, how many people are fed.

Outcome-based education is like a drinking glass. It is a structure into which educators can pour content. If the content is simply removed from the traditional container and poured into a new one, there will be little real improvement of student learning.

The future of outcome-based education will take one of two paths. One possibility is that it will go by the wayside because the structural change it requires is too massive for the entire system of education to handle. OBE in its ideal form would eliminate grade levels, traditional grading systems, classroom structures, and time allocations. While a single district can make such changes, graduating students must be able to enter colleges that recognize student achievement that does not conform to college credit. Colleges must, then, change their accreditation as well. OBE may die of its own ambitions.

Another alternative future is that the vision of outcome-based education will capture the attention of politicians who mandate that sweeping structural changes be made. This will mean a future of expanded federal and state control of education and an acceleration of the move away from local control.

15
The Feds Are Coming!

T HE PROBLEM WITH making education more political is that politics can change rapidly and radically—witness the 1994 Republican
victory in Congress. The *Goals 2000* program may be cut by Republicans. Consequently, you can read this chapter in one of two ways: (1) as a
critique of what *is* happening in education from the federal government,
or (2) as an example of what the federal government *wanted* to do with
education. Either way, it is instructive to examine the grand schemes of
the social engineers.

As if the problem in education is not already too many cooks planning too many meals for our teachers to serve and our children to eat,
federal bureaucrats ambitiously plan for our nation's schools to meet
eight specific goals by the year 2000. I'm not sure why the year 2000
was chosen except that it seems to hold some special allure. Everyone
talks about needing "the skills for the twenty-first century" as if workers on January 1, 2000, will need something different from what they
needed on December 31, 1999. Certainly, job skills change as business
and industry changes. A good education provides a foundation for a
person to adapt as his or her environment requires. However, no one
seems to challenge the arbitrary and impossible target of the year 2000
for the kind of changes federal planners call for.

The magic allure of 2000 aside, federal planners established for the 1990s an education version of what Kennedy established for the space program in the 1960s—an ambitious goal that captured the imagination of the country and gave focus to a particular endeavor. (It is telling that the growth of government is reflected in the fact that Kennedy had only one goal—a man on the moon by the end of the decade—while President Clinton outlined eight goals for education.) It quickly becomes apparent that the differences between education and aeronautical engineering are enormous: (1) NASA didn't have over 2.5 million employees who each had his or her own idea about how to get to the moon, (2) Education is hardly a science, and (3) NASA scientists didn't have to worry about such complicating factors as lazy students, incompetent and unmotivated families, and, in general, people who just refused to be as neatly controlled as social engineers would like.

The eight national goals are as unrealistic as they are ambitious. It's not that these goals are unworthy; it's that it is unrealistic to think they can be accomplished by the year 2000 and reaching them will not depend upon some federal government program:

1. By the year 2000, *all* children in America will start school ready to learn.

2. By the year 2000, the high school graduation rate will increase to at least 90 percent.

3. By the year 2000, *all* students will leave grades 4, 8, and 12 having demonstrated competency over challenging subject matter including English, mathematics, science, foreign languages, civics and government, economics, arts, history, and geography, and *every* school in America will ensure that *all* students learn to use their minds well, so they may be prepared for responsible citizenship, further learning, and productive employment in our Nation's modern economy.

4. By the year 2000, the nation's teaching force will have access to programs for the continued improvement of their professional skills and the opportunity to acquire the knowledge and skills needed to instruct and prepare all American students for the next century.

5. By the year 2000, United States students will be first in the world in mathematics and science achievement.

6. By the year 2000, *every* adult American will be literate and will possess the knowledge *and* skills necessary to compete in a global economy and exercise the rights and *responsibilities* of citizenship.

7. By the year 2000, every school in the United States will be free of drugs, violence, and the unauthorized presence of firearms and alcohol and will offer a disciplined environment conducive to learning.

8. By the year 2000, every school will promote partnerships that will increase parental involvement and participation in promoting the social, emotional, and academic growth of children.[1]

It is good to have goals. But, short of a totalitarian state, these goals cannot be reached. The federal government cannot control all the elements that would ensure success. But it will try. Let's look more closely at a few of the goals, specifically, goals 1, 2, 3, 4, and 8.

Goal 1

If *all* students *will* start school ready to learn, the government will have to control all families' nutrition and their children's nurture. The *Goals 2000* law directs states to "establish, expand, and operate" programs in which state social workers guide parents from the birth of their children until they enter school. These are voluntary programs, and the law clearly establishes that no parent will be forced to participate. Still, it lays the groundwork for every school district in the country to provide state workers to deliver—like pizza—state-approved parenting guidance to the home. These workers are to make "regularly scheduled personal visits with the families" and give "regularly scheduled developmental screenings" for the children.

While it is certainly true that many parents need guidance on how to be better parents, it is disquieting that this job is being filled by the state rather than by informal familial, church, or fraternal activities. In essence, the state is attempting to be a surrogate grandmother or aunt, guiding the new mother in how to raise her children. The takeover of child-rearing guidance by the state will further erode a sense of responsibility by extended family, local churches, or other informal societies that traditionally served to help raise children.

Just as federal welfare programs have had the effect of shifting charity from the private sector to the public, so these "pro-family" government programs will have a similar long-term effect. For instance, between 1935 and 1981 welfare given by private charities dropped from making up more than half of all aid to less than 1 percent.[2] Similarly, social security has had the effect of discouraging personal savings for retirement and children's sense of responsibility for the care of their parents. As George Gilder writes:

> The defenders of the welfare state at its current level usually seem to assume that without the public systems the sick, the poor, the elderly, and the youth would be left to their own devices; that the welfare state has a massive effect on the condition of the needy, but little impact on their willingness and ability to fend for themselves. Much evidence, however, indicates the opposite: that the programs have surprisingly little beneficial effect, but they do have a dramatic negative impact on motivation and self-reliance.[3]

In essence, goal 1 will result in turning schools into dispensers of welfare programs. *Goals 2000* clearly mandates that "state and local education improvement efforts must incorporate strategies for providing all students and families with coordinated access to appropriate social services, health care, nutrition, and early childhood education, and child care to remove preventable barriers to learning and enhance school readiness for all students."[4]

Goal 2

Concerning goal 2—graduation rates of 90 percent—one of three things will have to happen to see success: All teachers will have to rise to the quality of "Teachers of the Year" to help students succeed (un-likely), or graduation dates will have to be flexible so some students can graduate at age twenty-eight (impractical), or rigorous classes will have to be watered down to keep unmotivated students in school (prob-able). Overall, the graduation rate in 1993 was at 87 percent. Reaching the goal is in sight but is frustratingly elusive. Still, graduation rates *have* increased somewhat over the years, and there is hope. However, the temptation will be to make academics softer and increase the bent toward feel-good approaches since the most frequently cited reasons for dropping out are: "did not like school," "felt I didn't belong," "could not keep up with schoolwork," and "was failing school."[5]

A recent study found that teachers often compensate disadvantaged students' poor grades on homework and tests by also taking into con-sideration class participation, journal writing, lab work, and effort. These low-achieving students receive better grades than they otherwise would have because teachers consider these nonacademic factors.[6] These students may graduate, but they will not meet goal 3.

Goal 3

It is hard to imagine that within the short time remaining until the year 2000 there will be the drastic improvement in academics that federal plan-ners hope for. For instance, for the six years between 1984 and 1990 there was no change in students' writing proficiency; in fact, eighth-graders' skill actually declined slightly.[7] Is it realistic to believe that in the six years be-tween passage of the *Goals 2000: Educate America Act* in 1994 and the year 2000 there will be the massive increase in proficiency the bill calls for?

For the nineteen years from 1971 to 1990 the reading proficiency of all seventeen-year-olds improved only slightly, and in 1992, the percentage of high school seniors who met the federal planners' performance stan-dards ranged from 16 percent for blacks to 43 percent for whites.[8] Blacks and Hispanics made encouraging gains from 1980 to 1990. However, even if these strong gains continue from 1990 to 2000, both groups would still be below the average reading proficiency of whites who are themselves well below the hopes of *Goals 2000*. Still, the federal government imag-ines that by the year 2000 *all* students will demonstrate competence.

Most disturbing about goal 3 is that it requires all students to have multicultural education and health education. As we have already seen, this can translate into indoctrination of values radically different than those that parents endorse.

The federal government is prohibited by the Tenth Amendment from dictating curriculum content to states. However, the U.S. Department of Education has gotten around this by tying funding to compliance. Thus, conformity to government dictates is "voluntary" but carries with it financial rewards for compliant states.[9]

Goal 4

Goal 4 addresses teacher training. While it is essential that teachers be trained in the best ways to help students learn—and Congress makes provision for this—it also wants teachers trained in the "variety of educational, social, and health needs" of students.[10] This is a green light for those educators who are either unwilling or unable to separate academics from therapy. For instance, in a popular magazine for educators a teacher wrote an article on writing instruction subtitled, "How writing can help children feel more secure at school." This teacher suggests that her colleagues should have the students sit around and discuss "hypothetical situations that are anxiety-producing for kids" and then have them write solutions. This sort of group therapy could easily pass as an English lesson if schools are not careful.

Many schools of education already train teachers, not in how to teach their academic subjects, but in how to teach a feeling—be it a peace-oriented feeling, a multicultural feeling, a gender-neutral feeling, or a self-esteeming feeling. But these feelings are couched in academic-sounding terms such as social studies, home economics, and English.

For instance, a professor of education at Michigan State University comments that the aim of social studies "is for children to learn about themselves." He leads the teaching students in discussions about the inadequacies of textbooks to "properly" cover the effects of acid rain, nuclear weapons, and American bigotry.[11] Rita Kramer, author of *Ed School Follies*, visited schools of education around the country and found student teachers working harder at making America a more egalitarian society than a more academically accomplished one. For instance, an instructor at Teachers College at Columbia University teaches, "We have to educate this country for peace through cooperative learning."[12] I thought cooperative learning was promoted by educators for being academically better not politically better!

A conference sponsored by the California Association for the Education of Young Children, attended by five thousand preschool and elementary teachers, included workshops on "Affirming Lesbian and Gay Families with Young Children," "Earthbased Spirituality, Deep Ecology, Native Wisdom: What Do These Traditions Mean to Me?" and "How One School Improved the Quality of Their Program by Eliminating Traditional Holiday Celebrations."[13]

Unfortunately, this is the direction teacher training has headed for several years and, by all indications, there will be more of it in the future.

Goal 8

Goal 8 sounds good: By the year 2000, every school will promote partnerships that will increase parental involvement and participation in promoting the social, emotional, and academic growth of children. However, the language of the bill tends to imply that such partnerships have more to do with parents getting on board with schools than they do with schools listening to parents. This goal will most likely mean more social-welfare programs to meet "the varying needs of parents." Congress made sure it included the right language about "shared educational decision making" with parents and having parents "hold schools and teachers to high standards of accountability." But there is little likelihood that schools will be more responsive to parental concerns about curriculum, textbooks, and activities in the year 2000 than they are today. As local control of education continues to shift to state and federal levels, and as unions shield incompetent teachers from consequences, parents have little means for holding schools and teachers accountable for anything.

Rita Kramer observed a professor at Teachers College tell student teachers what to do when parents complain that their children aren't being taught phonics: "Her answer to that one brought down the house. 'Don't *tell* them you don't teach phonics,' she said. Then [she] added,

'You do.' They all smiled and nodded, as though they understood quite well what she meant."[14]

This is the sort of thing that drives parents crazy and drives them away from schools. Former Secretary of Education William Bennett observes how this has already happened: "Increasingly, parents became alienated or disenfranchised from their schools and yielded to the cult of 'expertise,' the authority of superintendents, 'education judges' or administrative bodies. And, as the teachers tell us, more and more parents dropped their children at the doorstep of the school and were gone to pursue their own interests."[15]

Though *Goals 2000* includes a place for parents, the effect of the whole law moves education away from parents. School administrators will most likely interpret goal 8 of the law to mean school-to-community public relations to support the federal- and state-directed programs.

A National School Board

To accomplish the eight federal goals for schools, the government has set up new politically pregnant bureaucracies. The first one is the National Education Goals Panel. Its eighteen members serve under the president. As if education is not political enough, the goals panel will be evenly split between Democratic and Republican politicians—not educators. Its purpose is to set national goals and approve what the second committee develops.

The second bureaucratic committee is the National Education Standards and Improvement Council. All nineteen members are appointed by the president with seven recommended by his secretary of education, four recommended by the Speaker of the House, four by the majority leader of the Senate, and four by the goals panel. Its purpose is to develop specific content standards and make sure states conform to its dictates.

The Vermont commissioner of education referred to the *Goals 2000* law as "a radically different federal role in education." He went on to explain, "The Goals Panel will set the goals, the Standards and Improvement Council will certify the standards to measure progress towards the goals, and the Secretary will oversee a state and local planning process to reach the goals." He expressed alarm that the law "will assert federal oversight over the whole educational program in a state or community."[16]

The national standards for teaching American history is a good example of how "government-approved knowledge" can be used to shape a generation's perception of our country. The final draft of the standards made no mention of the first gathering of the U.S. Congress, but its authors made sure students learned about the founding of the Sierra Club and the National Organization for Women. The standards didn't call for teaching about the Constitution and made one mention of Abraham Lincoln's Gettysburg Address. While it made nineteen mentions of the evils of McCarthyism and seventeen mentions of the Ku Klux Klan, it only mentioned Ulysses Grant once and never mentioned Robert E. Lee. Colonial life was viewed from a feminist perspective, making no mention of the faith that held these families together. While Margaret Sanger, founder of Planned Parenthood, was held up with esteem, the authors encourage students to put John D. Rockefeller on trial posthumously for crimes against "the common welfare."[17]

The national board also has the potential for telling teachers how to teach as well as what to teach. It will set standards for "how the content area can be most effectively taught."[18] And, just to keep its options open, the law allows for "other factors that the Council deems appropriate."[19] To allay people's fears that this represents a federal takeover of education, the law uses the word "voluntary" liberally. However, upon deeper reading it becomes clear that federal dollars are the reward for states who volunteer to participate.

Senator Judd Gregg anticipates that it won't be long before any federal money to states for education will be tied to compliance with federal standards. In arguing against the bill he warned, "One can expect that when this initiative is up and running, obtaining so much as a nickel in federal funds for current programs, such as for special education, will likely require compliance with the performance and content standards that have been certified by NESIC under this act."[20]

A basic problem that federal planners seem blind to is that the very act of trying to control the education process at the federal level mitigates against the success of the process. John Kincaid of the University of Washington points out, "Virtually all of the factors most associated with academically effective education are school- and neighborhood-based. Yet we have shifted more control and financing of education to state and national institutions."[21] Still, the planners sharpen their pencils and plan more.

Tests with No Teeth

A bewildering part of *Goals 2000* is the way it assesses progress toward its ambitious goals. States can voluntarily develop testing to assess student progress in conformity with the national content standards, and those tests can be certified by the National Education Standards and Improvement Council. According to a U.S. Department of Education official, the certification carries no weight but is "a type of Good Housekeeping Seal of Approval."[22] However, to receive the council's certification the state cannot use the results of its tests for graduation requirements, grade promotion, or retention of students until 1999—just one year before the eight national goals are to be met.[23] In other words, if the state develops its own test to measure how well students are achieving national content standards, and it puts teeth into the test by making it a tool for determining graduation and grade promotion or retention at any time before 1999, the national council will not certify it. A type of "Catch-22" occurs in which either the federal government actually discourages states from putting teeth in their tests, or the states ignore the federal government's certification of their tests.

Worse yet, *Goals 2000*, through its maze of funding incentives, actually encourages states not to use tests for purposes of graduation or grade promotion until 1999. The law authorized $400 million in grants to schools in 1994 as well as a wide-open wallet for "such sums as may be necessary" each year to 1998. However, to get the money a state must agree to report each year on the progress it is making in reaching state standards that are aligned to national standards. This requires testing students. The law also allows the federal government to give grants to states to help them in the design and administration of those tests. But if the state accepts that money, the test "developed and evaluated with funds under this section may not be used for decisions about the individual students relating to program placement, promotion, or retention, graduation, or employment" until 1999.[24] In other words, it has no teeth. The only way for a state to avoid this requirement while still being able to receive federal dollars authorized by *Goals 2000* is to pay for its own testing and report the results to the U.S. Department of Education.

Opportunity-to-Learn Standards

Goals 2000 requires what it calls "opportunity-to-learn" standards. These will be standards set by the national board for supposedly ensuring that all students have an equal opportunity to learn well. Under this provision the national board will set standards for the quality of curriculum and instructional materials in each classroom, all teacher qualifications, all teacher training, every class's conformity to national standards, how well all schools foster gender equity, and, of course, "other factors that the Council deems appropriate to ensure that all students receive a fair opportunity" to learn.[25] States will not be forced to comply with the board's standards. Sounds reasonable. However, there are problems on the horizon.

National opportunity-to-learn standards will mean more regulations created due to special-interest lobbies. For instance, *Goals 2000* ties its funding to state compliance with using "gender equitable and multicultural materials." To receive funding states must even demonstrate that teachers are using "gender-equitable methods" of teaching. One of the biggest impositions on states will be that they must develop plans for "increasing the access of all students to social services, health care, nutrition, related services, and child care services, and locating such services in schools, cooperative service agencies, community-based centers, or other convenient sites designed to provide 'one-stop shopping' for parents and students."[26] While the federal government will not dictate how to comply, it will use funding as an incentive for states to develop standards in areas the federal government wants.

John Hood, research director for the John Locke Foundation, points out, "Equity reforms do everything that research says is wasteful and counterproductive: redistribute funds from rich to poor districts; increase centralized state control over curriculum and management; and focus public and government attention on teacher's salaries, class sizes, and per pupil spending."[27] Opportunity-to-learn standards will also put schools and students at risk of faddish programs such as the exaggerated alarm over asbestos in schools, which redirected millions of dollars from education to asbestos removal. In hindsight, concern over asbestos was inflated, but the money was already spent.

Student-teacher ratios is another example of how good—even seemingly logical—intentions can have little effect and cause unintended harm. The conventional wisdom is that reduced class size translates into improved education. However, the U.S. Department of Education found that "the relationship between standardized test scores and class size is erratic at best and typically inconsistent with the thesis that smaller class sizes lead to higher achievement."[28] The trend for many years has been a reduction in class size nationwide at the same time average achievement has also declined. The school district with the smallest number of pupils per teacher is the District of Columbia, yet it ranks forty-ninth among states in SAT scores. Utah has the biggest classes in the country and is ranked fourth in the nation for SAT scores.[29] Yet the education establishment—which will have the ear of the national board—consistently pushes reduction of class size as a much-needed improvement for schools. This will increase the number of teachers (increasing the number of dues unions can collect) and severely increase the cost of education while shifting funds from other needed areas.

Opportunity-to-Learn Learning

Economist Eric Hanushek, along with twelve other economists, analyzed the cost of education to its performance and concluded: "Contrary to conventional wisdom, little systematic relationship has been found between school resources and student performance. Any findings showing that increases in basic school resources promote higher achievement are balanced by those showing the opposite."[30]

In Kansas City, a 1986 court order to improve the public schools there led to a stratospheric $1.2 billion spent in the Kansas City school district. The schools there are, by far, the best constructed and supplied in the country. Taxpayers built new schools with Olympic-sized pools and indoor running tracks. Thousands of computers fill the classrooms throughout the district. First-graders go to a computer lab where each child has his or her own terminal. Central High School has a robotics lab and a network of eight hundred computers—the largest in any American school. Teachers received large raises and sparkling new class-rooms with a maximum of twenty-five students per class. The district has magnate schools each having a different emphasis. One school is a foreign-language immersion school, another specializes in the fine arts, and another focuses on media communications where students produce their own television shows. There are fifty-six magnate schools in all.[31]

But despite all the spending and innovation, academic achievement has barely improved. In fact, junior and senior high school test scores were at the same level in 1994 as they were before the massive spending in 1984—and well below the national averages. Compared to other ur-ban areas such as Detroit and Los Angeles, Kansas City students are falling further behind.[32]

One school in the district has done well. Martin Luther King Middle School didn't get all the fancy equipment other schools got. The exist-ing building was merely spruced up. What it has that is different from other Kansas City schools is an emphasis on a basic curriculum; stu-dents wear uniforms, and parents sign a contract pledging to get their kids to school and help them with homework.[33] It wasn't the new things that made the difference at this school; it was the old things—strong curriculum, discipline, and parental responsibility.

One problem with trying to handle education at the federal level is that the process is cumbersome and political, and the result is too often negative. One education analyst comments, *Goals 2000* looks more like 2,000 goals. The combination of talking about "world-class standards" and having committees of experts design content goals results in three-ring binders full of standards that few teachers could meet, let alone their students. On paper it looks impressive, but as one teacher put it, "I already feel like I'm trying to stuff a ten-pound sausage in a five-pound bag."

Part Three
Becoming Schools Again

All children can be taught. Poor education is caused by poor teaching, and poor teaching is too often what children get.

Thaddeus Lott, principal

16
Encouraging Signs

THADDEUS LOTT IS an unreasonable man. Or at least that's what many of his colleagues used to believe. He is a principal who wants—no, demands—results. While the mantra of educators across the country is, "All children can learn," Lott cuts across the grain with his educational philosophy: "All children *can be taught.* Poor education is caused by poor teaching, and poor teaching is all too often what children get. The factor that will make the difference is good leadership; leadership that insists children learn, that is not afraid to use its authority to make sure they learn." Strong words for a man whose students are mostly poor minorities in Houston, Texas. Yet he gets results. His elementary students consistently score among the top students throughout the school district. Many of his first-grade students read at the third-grade level, and some read fifth-grade material. Many of his fifth-graders do eighth-grade math.

"I believe children can do a lot," he says. "Once you get them into a setting where they feel like they can, and they know you believe in them, they rise to the occasion. We have too many people who have low expectations of children, too many people who really don't think that children have the brains or ability to learn. The truth about them is that they can learn, and that's what we've proven."[1]

To create the right setting for learning, Lott demands much from his teachers. Many of them work twelve-hour days in lesson preparation and rehearsal as well as grading papers. At Wesley Elementary, where Lott is principal, students' work is graded every day so they have immediate feedback on their progress. He not only demands that students demonstrate good penmanship, but he monitors teachers' penmanship, as well. Modeling excellence is important to him.

When he took over Wesley Elementary in 1975 many of the teachers quit or chaffed under his rigorous demands. Those who stuck with him saw the value in his clear focus and high standards. His standards for teacher performance include working on the chalkboard every day, interacting with students during each lesson, assigning homework regularly, and grading all assignments promptly.[2] Teachers constantly monitor student progress and work with them until they master a skill. "We can no longer carry people who are not productive," explains Lott. "We are in competition with the world and we've got to be accountable for our students." Teachers who can't teach well should get new training to do it right or they should "hit the door."[3]

He doesn't accept excuses some people give for low-income minority students' failure. He tells students, "When you leave this campus you'll still be black, you'll still be poor, but you are going to be an independent learner."[4]

His most controversial approach is his use of phonics. Wesley teachers use the DISTAR program, which uses repetitive drills on letter sounds and the sounds of letter combinations to learn words. Teachers follow a script and encourage students to call out answers. Often all the students in a class will answer the teacher's question in loud unison. This rigid and disciplined style has turned many critics on Lott's approach. Education professors who advocate a whole-language approach with its emphasis on learning to read by combining it with writing, listening, and speaking, accuse Wesley teachers of stifling students' creativity and thinking skills. They claim the repetitive drills are demeaning to students and too much work for teachers.

This makes Lott's blood boil. "People are practicing educational genocide on minority students when they continue to use strategies that are not working. They never bring you anything that works better, but they criticize you for what you're doing. If what we're doing is working and you only have to have eyes to see, then I really don't care about the way someone feels about what I'm doing."[5]

George Bernard Shaw once wrote, "The reasonable man adapts himself to the world; the unreasonable one persists to adapt the world to himself. Therefore all progress depends on the unreasonable man."[6] Thaddeus Lott is an unreasonable man, and his students are grateful that he is.

We Should All Be "Unreasonable"

The key to survival in the future of public education (if there is a future for public education as we know it) is not to merely adapt to our troubled environment. We needn't accept the breakdown of families, the loss of decency, the shirking of responsibility, and the habit of laziness.

We needn't *adapt* to the problems of students when we attempt to teach character with value-neutral discussions. Our adaptation won't solve the problem. Only educators who take the leadership to train students in the convictions we as a society agree are right will solve the problem. Concerning matters on which we disagree, teachers need to lean toward conserving traditional morals and social standards. Those parents who want something more liberal can teach those things to their children outside the public system that everyone else's children are compelled to attend.

We needn't *adapt* to the breakdown of family and community by turning our schools into "one-stop shopping" centers for social-welfare programs. Our accommodation will not solve the problem. Only educators and community leaders who refuse to accept parental irresponsibility and demand greater initiative on the part of parents will begin to solve the problem. We must demand that our political leaders stop creating disincentives for families who want to take responsibility for their lives. Public education needs more "unreasonable" men and women in the public schools who will make a positive difference everyday.

Leadership in the Classroom

Larry Cuban, professor of education at Stanford University, makes a noteworthy observation: "National policymakers have yet to learn the fundamental lesson that the official curriculum—what is on paper—is not the same as what teachers do in the privacy of their classrooms."[7] In the end, that's what it always comes down to—good teachers who love their students and teach them well. And that is why the federal planners will fall short of their ambitions. Education takes place in classrooms, not congressional committees. At the national level conservatives will battle the federal government's dictating of standards and liberals will battle for the rights of underprivileged students not to have to reach federal standards. While the battle rages on, good teachers will do as they have always done—teach . . . and hope that the social engineers stay out of their way.

Bennett comments, "Seeing outstanding schools in action makes it clear why they succeed: local people, leadership, community commitment, and shared values, not federal tutelage. . . . [T]he 'system' doesn't educate anyone. Individuals do."[8] Individual teachers must make an important decision each day—a decision to help their students perform with excellence. Incompetence and ignorance are our natural states. No one comes into this world skilled and knowledgeable. For that each person must be trained and taught. And that requires hard work on everyone's part—students, teachers, principals, and parents. There is no federal program that can substitute for personal responsibility at the local level in classrooms and homes. This does not mean a cold indifference to students' problems. It means that parents and the community must pull together to solve those problems. It means local businessmen offering scholarships for graduates rather than federal grants. It means parents helping other parents when teens begin to wander from the straight and narrow. It means schools that have a clear mission of academic achievement and character development born from the values expressed by parents in the district. In short, it means authentic community made by a commitment to solving problems together rather than being merely a group of people who live near each other but depend upon the state or federal government hundreds or thousands of miles away to solve their problems.

There is a popular proverb educators like to refer to that states, "It takes a village to raise a child." In many education circles, unfortunately, the "village" has come to mean government rather than a close-knit community of people. The crisis in education occurs in large part because we allow our children to become the responsibility of others outside our "village" of our family, church, and neighborhood support system. The answer to the problem lies in taking back personal responsibility for our children and their futures. The answer won't be found at the federal level or even at the local level, but at the personal level.

Values in Action

What Thaddeus Lott is doing academically with students, Gene Bedley is doing morally with students—providing strong leadership. Bedley is an elementary school principal in the upper-middle-class city of Irvine, California. Over the last fifteen years, while garnering recognition as the PTA's National Educator of the Year, recipient of the National Principal's Award, and California's top educator award—The Keeper of the Dream—he has developed a character-education program like none in the country.[9] Though his school sits in the middle of a community of upwardly mobile baby boomers, he points out that these "overprivileged" families have as many, though differing, problems as those from low-income neighborhoods. "The negative impact of underprivilege and overprivilege can be equally as great," he says. Many of these two-income families don't see themselves as teachers, don't take time with their kids, don't give them a quiet place to study, don't give them proper nutrition, don't make learning a priority, and only see school as a means to a career.

His office reflects his personality—the desk shoved against one wall creating an unobstructed open space between his chair and the ones for students and parents. Soft-spoken but with a razor-sharp clarity about what he believes makes a good school, Bedley stresses good values as the starting point for all education.

His greatest lament about how parents raise their children? "I think most parents have not taught their kids respect. Respect is not manners. A child might have the habit of saying 'Yes, sir,' but that is not respect. Respect is not tolerance. If we confuse that we set ourselves up for problems. I can respect diversity, but I don't have to tolerate everything. Tolerance is 'putting up with,' and that is not the same as respect.

I show respect by listening to another opinion. I don't interrupt them. But it doesn't mean I agree with them. It involves a respect for classmates, a respect for teachers, a respect for the learning process. I think respect is so important that if that were taken care of everything else would be taken care of, too."

Bedley has developed a workshop on respect that each student in his school goes through. Teachers instruct the students about the importance of respect and lead the students through the process of how respect is put into action each day.

Bedley practices what he preaches. He goes to extraordinary lengths to include parents in their children's education. He communicates with parents through letters, newsletters, and meetings. When he discusses a behavior problem with a child, he will often record the session and send the tape to the child's parents. This, he finds, helps the parents understand the process of how to deal with inappropriate behavior. "The tapes give parents an opportunity to hear another parent work with the child through a problem. For parents who are ineffective this is a very effective technique. I can't be that child's parent, but I can assist the parents in how to take on their responsibility," Bedley comments. This is a center of Bedley's philosophy—being a resource for parents as they exercise their responsibility, not taking it from them.

"Parents are in trouble today. There are very few that are doing it right. They don't know the basics. Parents often ask teachers for help. They'll say, 'I don't know what to do with my child. Do you have any ideas?' That didn't happen when I started teaching years ago."

In what would be considered unusual for other schools but is in keeping with Bedley's style, he sent letters to the parents of students who exhibited good personal characteristics asking them what they do to raise good children. From their responses he developed a booklet he sent to all the parents with children in his school. He specifically looked at four areas: Personal responsibility, critical-thinking skills, positive attitudes, and internal motivation. (We'll look at the parents' responses in the next chapter.)

Bedley also solicits from parents information about their children that can help him decide in which class to place each child. "We don't ask the parent which teacher they want their children to have. We ask them what qualities they think their children need in a teacher." Bedley uses a seventeen-point criteria for determining where a child should be placed. "Of all the things I do as a principal, I think it's the most important thing to them—who their kids get as a teacher. I spend hours on this."

This is in keeping with emerging research on what impacts student learning. Edward Pauly, a senior research associate with Manpower Demonstration Research Corporation, reveals the conclusion of his research on school improvement:

> Our discovery documented an important and powerful truth: a student who attends a particular school is not educated in the whole school; he or she is educated in particular class-rooms *within* that school. A school and its policies do not necessarily determine its students' educational experiences. The distinction between school and its classrooms is crucial; teaching and learning take place in individual classrooms, which can easily differ from each other.[10]

Thaddeus Lott and Gene Bedley demonstrate that ultimately the answer lies not in government action, but in personal action. Policy-makers don't teach students. Schools don't even teach students. Teachers teach. And policies that promote and reward personal responsibility are the best course of action.

More Encouraging Examples

While the majority of those in the education establishment con-tinue to assume greater responsibility for raising children, there are hopeful signs that an opposite trend is also emerging.

Some school districts are becoming more parent-friendly and re-specting the rights and responsibilities of parents. As an example of this I think of Wicomico County School District in Salisbury, Mary-land. The district started a series of workshops called "Parents Can Make the Difference." If we want parents to be more responsible, we can offer them suggestions and expect them to be more responsible. Wicomico educators respond to the needs of busy parents, not by taking on the parenting responsibility but by accommodating parents' busy schedules. School personnel conduct six parenting-skills sessions in corporate lunchrooms where many school parents work. Local companies work with the district by allowing employees extended lunch hours. The program has been so successful that twenty companies now participate; more than three hundred parents have attended the work-site seminars on discipline, children's self-esteem, academic success, parent-child communication, and drug-free lifestyles. Adapting to the needs of the parents without trying to replace the parents is the key.

If we want parents to participate more in the school district, we need to reward that involvement by truly listening and acting on their concerns. A district doing just that is the Cherry Creek school district in Englewood, Colorado. School-board members there initiated "fireside chats" to reach more parents. Board members meet with parents in informal discussion sessions held at neighborhood schools throughout the sprawling district. Formal school-board meetings are too restrictive for real parent-board member dialog. District officials have found that more people attend the sessions as they open lines of communication and give parents meaningful interaction with board members.

While most policymakers seem to think that only a government program can solve community problems of students in poverty, one district is proving them wrong. Apache Junction Unified School District in Apache Junction, Arizona, has run an innovative charity program for the past twenty years called Project HELP. It is funded completely by donations and uses more than two hundred volunteers to run a food bank and clothing bank as well as emergency financial assistance for rent, utilities, and medical care. Instead of relying on a government program, the district serves as the catalyst to bring the community into charitable work. District employees can donate to Project HELP through payroll deductions, students run a canned-food drive twice each year, and local residents and businesses donate to support the program. If families need long-term help, they are referred to government agencies. This is an example of school officials seeing a need and providing leadership in calling local residents to reach out to their neighbors.

There are thousands of teachers who are fed up with the direction of public education. They are quietly resisting the Big Nanny syndrome behind the closed doors of their classrooms. A new organization has formed for the hundreds of thousands of public-school teachers who feel the liberal unions and other associations do not speak for them. The Association of American Educators is a refreshingly conservative alternative for these teachers. In its first year of operation, and with hardly any promotional budget, it has attracted nearly three thousand members.[11] Its goal is to have half a million members by the year 2000. Already it has attracted half a dozen national "Teachers of the Year." It offers a monthly newsletter, liability insurance, regional workshops, and an annual national convention for its members.

A growing number of educators are refusing to accept and accommodate the mediocrity they see. For instance, many schools are beginning to use character-education programs stressing clear and unambiguous ethical standards. Abstinence-based sex-education programs are gaining popularity, though they are still strongly resisted by those who favor promiscuity-based approaches (reflecting the philosophy, "We can't expect these kids to control themselves"). Still, the fact that there is a growing number of such programs available is encouraging.

The increasing involvement of parents is also an encouraging sign. They are breaking out of complacent PTA groups and starting their own, more conservative organizations. They are involving themselves in textbook selection, curriculum review, and school-district policy formulation. They are taking personal responsibility for the way their schools function, much to the frustration of educators stuck in the status quo.

Some parents have even taken the lead in starting charter schools within their districts. For instance, Dr. Randy Everett and his wife, Ruth Ann, along with other parents, submitted a proposal to the Fort Collins, Colorado, school board to start a more back-to-basics school. The district agreed to it and Washington Core Knowledge Elementary began. The school uses the Hirsch Foundation's Core Knowledge curriculum as well as state and local guidelines. It incorporates school-based management, a library developed through parental selection, tutoring by parents, a strong phonics reading program, encouragement to limit television viewing, and plenty of parent volunteers (six hundred volunteer hours per month). All these ingredients pay off. One teacher commented, "I've taught for several years, but this is the first time *all* my kids knew how to read by Christmas." Results like that caused parents to flock to the school. After only one year of operation, the waiting list to enroll was three times greater than the school's capacity.

The men and women, parents and teachers, in these districts are considered unreasonable by those who want to turn schools into orphanages. But it is exactly this kind of unreasonableness that is so encouraging. It shows people taking personal responsibility for their lives and for changing their world. It shows vision for how things should be rather than merely settling for what is. It shows the dignity and independence of the human spirit refusing to be smothered in the fat arms of the government.

17
Breaking the Orphanage Syndrome: A Paradigm Shift

A S WE HAVE SEEN, the programs and policies that are currently considered by the education establishment as "pro-family" often result in aggravating family problems. Schools have responded to the weakened family structure by expanding their areas of responsibility of child-rearing. This expansion of responsibility and centralization of function has the effect of narrowing the officially sanctioned options for parents.

For instance, within the school's walls there is one way to teach about sexuality or multiculturalism or self-esteem or any number of nonacademic subjects. The schools cannot possibly please everyone's viewpoints on these subjects. Consequently, schools are continually pitted against various community factions. These disputes can largely be eliminated if schools will reverse their present course of action. They can narrow, rather than expand, their mission to focus on academic subjects and leave the other subjects to privately funded efforts outside the school.

Many people within the education establishment assume that if the school does not provide a particular service, it won't be provided by anyone. However, this assumption fails to acknowledge two important points: (1) Once driven out of schools, the special interests that promote nonacademic subjects can and will find other opportunities to assist families who want their help; (2) If the service in question does fall by the wayside it will be because there was no desire by advocates to privately fund it, or there was no parent who found the service important enough to use. Either way, the value of the service will not be artificially sustained by schools. Ineffective and undesirable programs will be eliminated, and effective and desirable programs will still flourish outside the school system.

This calls for a significant paradigm shift in the mission and role of public education. The current paradigm, or model, for public schools is for schools to be *the* remedy for society's problems. If we are going to see major improvements in education, one important factor will need to be that schools must relinquish the notion that they are the centers for social welfare. This call for such a shift so cuts against the grain of the way we currently think about schools many within the education establishment will call it cruel and heartless. But this is because in their hearts they lack faith in the ingenuity and compassion of neighbors, churches, and community organizations. If we are to truly buttress the institution of the family while restoring the integrity of public education, there is no other course we can take.

Another aspect of the needed paradigm shift is to move schools to become the foundation for public progress, but not its vanguard. The predominant thinking by the education establishment is that society can best be changed by molding the minds of the next generation. This is the reasoning behind school missions that refer to helping kids have "proper" attitudes about global, multicultural, environmental, and sexual issues. The current vision is one in which schools cut the path that society follows. This, however, turns democracy on its head and inhibits America's conversation with itself about which direction it should take.

The idea that schools are the vanguards of social change has resulted in many high school graduates who can't think well enough to comprehend intricate sociopolitical editorials printed in the newspaper, but they certainly know where they should stand on the issues of global warming, reproductive freedom, and world peace.

Public education needs to shift from the vanguard paradigm to the foundation paradigm. Rather than trying to lead society on social issues, it should focus on providing the foundation for helping citizens enter public debate on issues as fully capable participants.

Social debate and change are adult activities requiring intelligent, adult participation. Schools would best serve society by giving students the intellectual tools to adequately enter the adult world of sociopolitical discussion. A high school graduate who has never discussed global warming but who is a proficient reader and a sharp thinker is better equipped to prepare for a serious discussion of the matter than is the graduate who has been indoctrinated with a position but who lacks the skills to investigate the issue for himself or herself.

If public education does not make a shift to a new paradigm of limited responsibility and foundational academics, the public will shift away from public education. This is already occurring in hundreds of communities around the country as various drives for parental choice of schools gain acceptance and momentum.

Though this book is not intended to be primarily about public policy, it does imply the direction that policies should go. Politicians, parents, and educators must begin discussing the limits of public education's mission and the need for greater parental responsibility. I offer the following suggestions in the hope that they will spur discussion and debate among educators, school board members, and legislators:

1. *Narrow the focus of schools to academic success and to fostering the academically necessary values needed to achieve that success.* Clarity of focus is one of the major problems of schools. It would be far better for schools to do one thing well rather than one hundred things poorly.

Schools should focus themselves on being the shapers of society in two areas—cognitive performance and basic, social character. With intellectual skills firmly in place, students will then be able to intelligently and competently enter into the public discourse that occurs *outside* of schools on political, religious, and social ideas. With a basic sense of character, a student can become a productive member of society. When it comes to the content of character education, schools should err on the side of being more conservative rather than "progressive." As the major institution that conserves and passes along our culture, schools should, by definition of function, resist the itch to alter cultural norms until society at large, having forged ideas of progress on the anvil of public debate, asks schools to do so.

2. *Cost-to-result analysis needs to be rigorously applied once clarity of focus is established.* Every expenditure for every program, purchase of material, or policy implementation needs to be tied very specifically to measurable academic results. If the cost of a new idea cannot be justified by measurable results, it should be discarded. Certainly, not every idea will prove effective, and many programs cannot be proven effective until they are tried. However, benchmarks are needed for unemotional analyzing of programs' effectiveness and disciplined elimination of those things that are ineffective. This rarely happens in schools today.

3. *Eliminate or severely reduce courses and programs that are nonacademic.* These include courses such as: sex education, multiculturalism, stress-reduction courses, drug and alcohol education, self-esteem courses, driver education, parenting education, decision making, consumer education, and sexual-harassment education. These subjects can be addressed in evening and weekend programs offered by for-profit and nonprofit organizations. If parents want their children to receive education in these subjects beyond what they can give them themselves, they can enroll their children in such programs offered by interest groups that advocate various agendas in those subjects. This creates a more democratic environment allowing parents real choices and responsibilities for the education of their children.

The issue is not whether these subjects are worthy of study but whether schools should be responsible for teaching them. Under this suggestion schools could still act as disseminators of information about the variety of programs available to parents and students in the community. Schools and public advertising can play a role in asserting moral persuasion for people to act privately. This may best be illustrated by the campaign of Mothers Against Drunk Drivers to make driving while intoxicated a shameful act. Through aggressive public relations they have made great strides in persuading the public of the immorality of one area of irresponsibility.

Currently, the most divisive subject taught in public schools is sex education. The classic answer given by educators when asked why schools teach sex education at all is that they do it because parents don't. The assumption is that if parents aren't fulfilling a responsibility, schools should. The better response that would help schools maintain clarity of focus is for public and private agencies to mount an advertising campaign that encourages parents to talk to their children about issues of sexuality, and for schools to inform parents of the privately funded programs available. This places responsibility back in the hands of parents.

The fundamental issue here, beyond the usurpation of parental responsibility, is parental rights. The conflict is not really about the rights of parents to restrict or direct their children's education versus the rights of the children to learn something. The real conflict is between the rights of parents versus the rights of education professionals who claim to know what is in the best interest of the children. Brigitte Berger of Wellesley College and Peter Berger of Boston University, in their book, *The War Over the Family*, highlight this point and urge readers to, "In general, trust parents over against experts; the burden of proof against individual parents should be very strong indeed before the opposite choice is made."[1]

4. *Schools need to resist, as much as possible, policies that put them in the role of welfare dispensers.* School-based health clinics should be removed. After-school day care for children should be dropped. All such programs divert schools away from an academic focus and remove family responsibilities from parents.

Concerning "intervention" programs to supposedly help the family, Brigitte Berger and Peter Berger write:

> Public policy with regard to the family should primarily be concerned with the family's capacity to take care of its children, its sick and handicapped, and its aged. The basic principle here should be that, whenever possible, these needs are best taken care of within the family—any family (barring a very few families to whom one would not entrust those who are weak or in need), regardless of social or cultural type. This means that the overriding concern of public policy should be to provide support for the family to discharge these caring tasks, rather than to relieve the family of these tasks.[2]

5.   *Of course, if schools are to relinquish the various parental responsibilities they have assumed over the years, there must also be in place policies that will encourage parents to resume their responsibilities.* Local, state, and federal policies should be enacted to encourage one parent to stay at home. Tax incentives could be created to encourage this. This wouldn't necessarily have to mean a push for one-income families exclusively. Government policies could be structured in such a way as to encourage home-based offices for corporate employees as well as entrepreneurs. The idea is to encourage one parent to be home when the children come home.

6.   *Schools should teach entrepreneurial skills to students in regular high school business classes as well as vocational education classes.* This kind of education empowers families to create their own jobs and equips students with the skills to contribute to family businesses run out of the home. For families who don't have their own business but who have one parent who works at home for a company, teenagers could contribute secretarial and clerical skills to support that parents' home-based office. Sociologist James Coleman points out, in referring to the nineteenth-century rise in public schooling:

> As men ceased working in or near the home, there came to be a social investment in a new, "constructive" institution, the school. Although the complex of changes that led to public schooling cannot be easily separated, certainly the fathers leaving home-based employment where their sons could learn adult work from them for corporation-based employment was a non-trivial element of this.[3]

Encouraging a parent to work from home and involve the child could foster both stronger work habits and greater emotional stability for the child. It would also give added value to child-rearing. In past generations children contributed economically to the well-being of the family by working on the farm or in the family business. It was to the parents' advantage to nurture their children because they were seen as investments that paid returns for the family while the children were growing up and later in support of the parents in old-age.

Today, children are largely a financial burden on parents who receive no return on their investment. The government has responded by developing programs to relieve parents of the burden, but this will only speed the irrelevancy of the family. Government policies must be instituted that promote the economic value of raising children.

7.   *Offer parent-information classes and seminars about school curriculum during the evenings and on weekends.* Pay teachers to conduct frequent seminars on what they are teaching in the classroom and how parents can work with their children. Work in conjunction with local businesses to reward parental attendance with coupons such as two-for-one dinner offers from local restaurants. In turn, the businesses' donations of products or services to the school are tax-deductible. This is an example of communities coming together to solve a problem of parental involvement.

Certainly it would be better if parents took the initiative to attend such meetings without financial incentives. But people who are irresponsible often need to be gradually trained to be responsible. People learn to be responsible by moving from external motivation to internal motivation. Rewarding parents may not be the best approach, but it is one idea that might help get things started.

8.   *Make schools more accessible to parents.* Keep students in neighborhood schools, and avoid busing them across town. Set up voice-mail homework messages so parents can call to get homework updates from teachers. Have more frequent open-house nights at schools so teachers can talk to parents about specific units of instruction rather than one night for the entire quarter or semester. Again, in conjunction with local businesses, use some type of incentive to reward parental participation.

9.   *Improve school-to-home communication.* Report cards should have more information in them to help parents understand their children's performance, and they should provide parents with ideas on how to help their children improve. Schools could expand report cards to be three or four pages of evaluations, comments, and subject-related parent tips for helping students. Teachers could use menu-driven computer programs to access prewritten paragraphs appropriate for almost any type of student evaluation. The technology exists to provide detailed evaluations and suggested courses of action for improvement.

And parents want this information. When sociologist Joyce Epstein of Johns Hopkins University surveyed parents regarding their desire to know what a letter grade represents about their children's progress, she concluded that "parents are very eager for this information." She went on to comment, "Parents at all economic levels, in all communities—urban, rural, and suburban—are asking, 'How do I help? What can I do? Where is the information I need?'"[4]

10. *Some system of choice is necessary to truly empower parents and place them at center stage in the education process.* The current structure of public schools sees families as clients rather than consumers. A client is someone who depends upon the services of another. A consumer is someone who acquires goods or services. A client denotes someone who is acted upon; a consumer denotes someone who acts. If we want parents to be more active in their children's education we must devise ways that turn the parents into consumers rather than clients.

When funding for education follows the child rather than the institution, the parent becomes an empowered consumer. Many middle- and upper-middle-income families have the option (often with great sacrifice) of choosing schools. They do this either by paying for private schools or moving to communities that have strong public schools. Low-income families have few options and remain clients of the public schools.

The paradigm shift from vanguard to foundation will take a courage that many politicians and educational leaders may find difficult to muster. Certainly, developers of nonacademic curriculum will resist this shift because it threatens their livelihood. Teacher union leaders will resist this because it threatens their agendas.

Educators like to speak of academic freedom for themselves. I propose that parents and students need academic freedom as well. They must be free to have the best academic education possible, free from unwanted indoctrination from self-appointed social engineers. Unfortunately, many parents will resist this. They have grown accustomed to being clients of public employees' nurturing. For them, freedom is a risk they are unwilling to take, a responsibility they are unwilling to accept. But if we are to progress toward academic freedom and family self-sufficiency we must do so on our own.

18
Becoming a Relevant Parent

I T IS EASIER to point the finger at the government for assuming too much responsibilities for families than it is for families to resume their responsibilities. Responsibility requires work. It means we must sometimes make tough choices about what we will do. It sometimes means giving up something we would *like* to do for something we *must* do. But it is a trap to think that the government is helping us when it relieves us of a parental task. What it is, in fact, doing by taking on such things is rendering the family irrelevant.

Here, then, is a general rule of thumb to live by: For the most part, avoid accepting from the government what you can do for yourself. Self-reliance is a virtue worth sacrificing for. To better understand the issue of reliance, picture a series of concentric circles with self-reliance in the center circle. When you have done all you can to solve a problem or provide for your family within that circle you must move outside of it to the next circle: family-reliance. One reason it is our responsibility to maintain strong ties to immediate and extended family is to provide support for ourselves when our own resources for self-support have run dry. Examples of family-reliant support include childcare, financial assistance, emotional support, and aid during sickness and old age.

When the limits of family-reliant support have been tapped (and sometimes in junction with family support) we can turn to neighborhood and community support. This often comes in the form of churches, temples, synagogues, service clubs, and privately funded charities.

These three areas of reliance—self, family, and community—are outside the realm of government. Government policies should focus on freeing up, strengthening, and even rewarding (through tax policies) the individual initiative required at each of these levels.

The fourth concentric circle is the start of government assistance. However, it begins at the most local level and works outward from the town or city to the county, to the state, and finally to the federal government.

It would be beneficial if government tax policies were structured in such a way that the rewards for moving away from self-reliance diminished at each level. Self-reliance should be the most generously rewarded, while turning to state and federal assistance should be the least. This would discourage families from jumping from self-reliance directly to governmental reliance while skipping familial and privately funded, community-based support systems.

Even in the face of current government policies that often have the effect of discouraging self-reliance and reliance on family, there are specific things you can do to take greater responsibility for your children's education. I offer the following suggestions as ways to avoid giving in to the lure of the public orphanage and, instead, to maintain parental control.

Things You Can Do As a School Parent

1. *Develop and maintain a close working relationship with your children's teachers.* Let it never be said that you use the schools as daycare for your children. Instead, view the teacher as a resource in your child-rearing network. Realize that just like any network needs maintenance, your relationship with your children's teachers needs frequent attention.

In my book *Creating a Positive Public School Experience*, I go into detail on exactly how to do this. Here, I will summarize the major ingredients for building and maintaining a strong parent-teacher relationship:

A. Find something the teacher has done that you appreciate and tell him or her so. Write a note of appreciation and mail it to the teacher using the school's address. Focus on something the teacher has done that has helped your child. Everyone enjoys compliments, and teachers rarely get them from parents. If you do this one simple gesture, you will go to the top of that teacher's list of "parents most worth listening to."

B. Volunteer to help in class. There are many opportunities for parents in elementary schools. You can still show a willingness to help at the secondary level by letting the teacher know you have a profession, hobby, or interesting experience that is related to the subject and that the class might like to hear about. Bankers can explain their profession to economics or business classes. Carpenters can explain their work to shop or drafting classes. Social workers can explain their work to health or social studies classes.

C. Be enthusiastic and positive about parent-teacher conferences. Dress professionally to make a good impression. Focus your discussions on constructive solutions to your child's needs. Share information about your child that will help the teacher as he or she teaches. Share the insights you have about what motivates your child and what sparks his or her interest. End the conference by asking the teacher what you can do to improve your child's performance, behavior, or attitude.

2.   *Obtain a list of academic goals from your child's teacher.* You will want to find out what knowledge and what skills your child will be expected to demonstrate by the end of the quarter, semester, or year. As you build your relationship with the teacher, you can also ask for the academic goals for individual units of instruction. Knowing these goals will help you work with your child at home and monitor his or her progress. If you sense that your child is not reaching the academic expectations, you can then alert the teacher and, together, develop a plan for corrective action.

3.   *Volunteer to start a parent support group within your child's school.* Meet with the principal and suggest that he or she allow you to conduct

meetings in a classroom during the evenings once a week for interested parents. This would not be a program run by the school. While the school could act as the catalyst for starting and promoting the support group, it would be parent-initiated and parent-led.

The parent support group would serve as a meeting place for small groups of parents to exchange ideas on motivating their children, handling homework, general parenting tips, and comfort and advice on dealing with children's behavioral problems.

4. *Start a parent-to-parent network.* You could help single parents, parents new to the community, and parents who don't have relatives or friends nearby with a network of school parents. This would be a parent-initiated program spurred on by the school's encouragement and help in getting the word out. In cooperation with the principal and other parents, devise a questionnaire to disseminate to parents. Of course, completing the questionnaire would be optional, and none of the questions should be of a sensitive nature.

Your goal is to start a file with the names of parents who are looking for another parent (or parents) to connect with. Each file would have voluntarily offered information on the parents' interests, number of children, concerns, and needs. The files would be used only for social connections between parents and would be available in the school office to any interested school parent. The connections between parents would be completely informal with no "programmed" commitments or expectations. The files could be considered similar to computer bulletin boards: people making connections to exchange information. The school office simply becomes the central processing system for the network.

This is one way for people to connect in our transient society. Friendships that develop through the network will help parents give and receive mutual support and advice.

5. *Set up a parent-mentoring program.* This could be initiated in the same way as the parent-to-parent network but with one important difference. The parent-mentoring program would encourage one parent to come alongside another parent who needs advice, encouragement, or assistance. You might start by asking for parents (or grandparents) who would volunteer to be mentors. You're looking

for experienced parents who could offer their experienced insights to other parents.

Once you have a few parents, get the word out that they are available to counsel any parent who needs help. The program would be informal. No "professional" training for the mentors is necessary. All this program is intended to do is use the school as a catalyst to restore a sense of neighborliness to your community. If you try to formalize it with training and curriculum or some such "institutionalizing," you will stifle the idea of neighbor helping neighbor and, instead, turn the mentor parents into social workers.

6. *Start a parent-run childcare program during parent-teacher conferences to make it easier for parents to attend.* Parents from the school could volunteer to conduct an activities program in the gymnasium for older children and supervise younger children in a makeshift nursery on campus.

7. *Ask the principal if you could help start a parent-resource room on campus.* This is a specially designated room you could stock with parenting magazines, books, and videos useful to parents. It should be a place where parents feel comfortable and welcome, where they are able to meet with other parents as well as check out materials.

8. *Edward Pauly's research on the importance of placing your child in the proper classroom means that you should take special steps to help determine which classroom your child will be in.* Pauly offers five suggestions for parents:

   A. Contact your child's school in early spring to determine when administrators will assign the next year's students to classrooms.

   B. Find out as much as you can about the teachers your child might have next year and the classmates he or she may be with. Network with other parents whose children have had these teachers. Visit the classrooms of next year's teachers and observe their style of teaching.

   C. Give the principal specific, written information about what you believe your child needs in next year's classroom. Does the child need more or less structure and discipline? Does he or she need higher expectations? Does he or she need to be separated from a classmate who caused significant problems for the child this year? Did the child do well with this year's algebra I teacher? Perhaps he or she needs to be with the same teacher next year for algebra II if the same teacher teaches it.

D. Provide the relevant family information that would help an administrator place your child in the appropriate class. Is there sibling rivalry that you could avoid? Did an older brother or sister have a particular teacher who was not effective and whom you would like this child to avoid?

E. Keep in mind that if the principal doesn't place your child in a classroom that will work for your child, you can have him or her changed. Be persistent in your requests. Be sure to give well-reasoned defenses for your judgments. Often persistence pays off. However, listen to the school staff, as well. They have insight into your child's performance at school that you might lack.[1]

Things You Can Do As a Citizen Parent

1. *Discuss with your local school-board members where the lines of responsibility should be drawn between schools and families.* Visit school-board members individually outside the official school-board meeting. In this more informal environment you will have more time to express your viewpoints, and the board member will feel more free to speak his or her mind. Your goal should be to build consensus on the board for greater academic focus and less encroachment on what should be family responsibilities.

2. *Volunteer to sit on school-district committees that are open to parental participation.* Use this position to express a "less-is-more" philosophy of school responsibility.

3. *Write to your local legislative representatives, both state and federal, and express concern that government is encroaching on the family in too many areas.* Be specific in what you don't like, and offer a constructive suggestion about how education can be improved.

Things You Can Do As a Parent at Home

1.   *Arrange your family finances to allow one parent to be home when your child is home.*

2.   *Take responsibility for teaching your child the nonacademic subjects that schools should drop from their curriculum.* Read books on sex education, self-esteem development, drug education, stress management, environmental awareness, respect for other cultures and people, and dating relationships.

Meanwhile, if your child is in a school that teaches these subjects, you will need to examine the curriculum. If you find the material offensive, you can respectfully ask that your child be removed from the lessons or you can use the lessons as an opportunity to teach your child discernment.

3.   *Build and maintain strong connections to your family.* Take responsibility for nurturing your primary social safety net: your family. While this is not a book on how to mend broken families, it is a call for people to reconnect and reaffirm the value of their families. If you find that you have some tears to mend in your family's fabric, I recommend you read a few books on how to do it or seek counsel from friends or even get professional help to do so.

4.   *Join a place of religious worship where you can nurture your "inner" person and where you can add to your social support network.* The presence of religious values in the home can have tremendously beneficial results in the lives of parents and children. Believing that we are addressed and examined by God expands our sense of responsibility to Him and to others.

At the same time, maintaining a weekly connection with friends who share common values creates a strong system of support for advice, comfort, and assistance in the many trials of life. Families who do not have this, I believe, are more vulnerable to falling in the face of life's many hardships.

5.   *Make a point of raising a responsible and achieving child.* Gene Bedley surveyed the parents of successful students to find out what they did to develop their children. You may find their responses to his questions helpful for your family.

A. What do you do to help your child become so responsible?

"We set up a system where the child earns tickets for responsible behavior and exchanges tickets for everyday privileges. It teaches our child to be responsible for her behavior and actions, both positive and negative."

"We try to help our son understand that once he makes a commitment to so something, it is important that he act responsible, follow through, and finish his undertaking with care and enthusiasm. After-school classes are an example. There are times during the eight-week session when he is tired or just doesn't want to attend. But we talk to him about his responsibility to himself and his teacher and classmates. After finishing the classes, he feels both pleased and satisfied that he has fulfilled his commitment and is proud of his accomplishment."

"We teach teamwork from birth. Everyone has chores; we all work until we can all rest. We believe the ability to perform all tasks creates independence. Our boy can cook and clean; our girls can mow a lawn."

"Our children have jobs to do, which become a routine to their lives (bathe, clear their own plates from the table, keep their rooms picked up). Also, when we are in public we always expect good behavior and don't settle for anything else."

"We teach our children that we are responsible for our own emotions. We 'own' them. Allow children choices and decisions. Overprotecting doesn't allow children to become responsible. Let them accept the consequences, good or bad."

"In our oriental customs, we make children consider teachers the same as their parents, or more than their parents. Children absolutely have to obey their teachers."

"From an early age, we allowed the children to make choices, with guidance if the choice was a major one, but on their own whenever possible. We also allow them a say in many of the decisions we make which involve the family."

"At about two and a half to three years old it was our son's responsibility to dress himself, hang up his pajamas, and wash his face, brush his teeth and comb his hair."

B. What do you do to help your child become so good at critical thinking?

"We often answer our children's questions with a directed question. If you answer a question with questions first to find out what exactly they are asking and second to make them come up with a probable answer themselves, this will open up the discussion and you will find the children can come up with many interesting possible answers themselves."

"We taught our son a step-by-step approach to problem solving. We do not do it for him. We have also noticed several times that if we agreed to help but waited awhile to do so, our son would go ahead and do things by himself that he thought he couldn't do without our help. If he really needs help, he is sure to ask again. We feel this teaches him persistence."

"We do not do our daughter's homework; neither do we solve her problems for her if we feel she can solve them herself. We also try to be a good example for her in modeling how we solve our problems."

"Our attitude about the importance of an education is very clear. It is not 'if you go to college' . . .We always say, 'When you go to college . . .'"

"We emphasize that homework comes before playtime. I also ask my son if he has all the necessary materials to complete his assignments. If he has forgotten anything we go back to school to get it. He then studies until his homework is completed. He can ask for help only after he has made several attempts to solve the problem himself. Even after he asks for help I only give him hints to get him on the right path."

"I read aloud to my child almost every night at bedtime for fifteen to thirty minutes. I read with expression and use different voices for various characters. I ask him questions about the story, and we discuss the story. I encourage him to ask me questions if he doesn't understand a word or concept. I also read nonfiction to him. This provides opportunities to talk about things in the world."

"We do a variety of things. We use computer adventure games that require problem solving. We play 'twenty questions' and word games when traveling in the car. We discuss the various ways to handle a hypothetical problem or situation. We go to places that are educational. We bring our kids to work and show them what we do. We ask for our children's input when we make family decisions."

C. What do you do to create such strong initiative and motivation in your child?

"Our daughter's high level of motivation comes from being expected to complete projects she is capable of doing."

"We give our daughter positive reinforcement for any task she completes successfully."

"Our child's ability to work independently seems to have come from our not pushing her academically when she was little. She was seven years old before entering first grade and did not start reading or spelling until then. But she requires little help or prodding from us to do her work."

D. What do you do to help your child have a positive mental attitude?

"We start off the day bright and cheerful and send the kids to school with, 'Try your best and study hard, for this day shall never come again.' We see our children off at the bus stop, wave good-bye, and meet them there when they come home by bus again whenever we can. It makes them happy to be met with hugs."

"In our home we frequently repeat what we call 'pearls': 'Inch by inch, everything's a cinch,' 'Bloom where you are planted,' 'Your mind is like a bucket of water; fill it with good thoughts and the bad ones spill out.'"

"We always support our girls' teachers. It is crucial to never talk against any teacher in front of your children."

"Each night as they go off to sleep I try to tell our children something positive and specific that I saw in them that day. We also speak highly of our children to others while they are present."

"Our favorite saying is, 'Never say I can't, always say I'll try.'"

This last bit of advice: "Never say I can't, alway say I'll try" is not only good for children to remember, it is good for us, as parents to remember as well. We must take greater responsibility for what we can do and try with all our ability to fulfill the responsibilities we might, at first, think we can't.

A Final Thought

Freedom can be scary. It carries a burden of responsibility. Freedom without responsibility results in social disorder and a bondage to those who *do* take responsibility for our lives. To truly be free requires us to be responsible. If we are to move boldly into the next century with confidence of a brighter future, we must regain our children's academic freedom to learn by regaining our responsibility for it. This does not necessarily mean we must home-school our children. On the other hand, public schools have expanded what they call "education" to include almost every aspect of raising children. With our busy schedules and our struggles to earn a living, it is tempting to accept this expanded view of education. However, this is not academic freedom, it is academic bondage.

As we have seen, a school teaches a subject with a single perspective. For instance, it offers one way to teach sex education, one way to teach multiculturalism. It endorses a specific value regarding the subject. There is little, if any, freedom for dissent. Those who do with any forcefulness are branded radical and divisive. This is not academic freedom, and often the subject is not even academic.

We, as a society, must decide what our public schools will be: institutions of learning or institutions for the care of children. We must decide whether our social and tax policies will truly be pro-family in helping the family be self-sufficient or whether our future will only be pro-family in that the raising of families is done by the pros—social workers, teachers, mental-health workers, and an army of other government employees.

We must decide whether we will have schools or orphanages.

Appendix

This list of organizations has been compiled to help you, your school, and your place of worship meet various community needs without using government programs. These groups may be able to help you directly; they may be able to help you provide information to your school; or, they may help you develop a supportive program for families within your community.

Character Education

National Association of Release-Time Christian Education
P.O. Box K
Ellijay, CA 30540
706-276-7900
This organization assists parents of children in public schools so they can arrange scheduled times for religious instruction off-campus during school hours. This release-time for religious education is in accordance with state laws that allow certain amounts of time for students to receive such instruction if requested.

The Thomas Jefferson Center
270 E. Foothill Boulevard, Suite 302
Pasadena, CA 91107
818-792-8130
   This organization produces values curricula for public schools. They also offer seminars and conferences.

Values In Action
14252 East Mall
Irvine, CA 92714
714-551-6690
This group produces K-6 values programs published by educator of the year Gene Bedley that are suitable for use in public schools.

Conservative Teachers' Organizations

Association of American Educators
26012 Marguerite Parkway, Suite 333
Mission Viejo, CA 92692
800-704-7799
   This nonpartisan association provides resources and encouragement to public school teachers holding conservative and moderate political and moral values.

Christian Educators Association International
P.O. Box 50025
Pasadena, CA 91115
818-798-1124
   This organization provides resources and encouragement for teachers in public schools.

Educational Choice

Independence Institute
14142 Denver West Parkway, Suite 101
Golden, CO 80401
303-279-6536
   This organization provides information on issues regarding school-choice plans to improve public education.

Center for the Study of Popular Culture
9911 W. Pico Blvd., Suite 1290
Los Angeles, CA 90035
310-843-3699
   This organization fights for conservative values in the entertainment media and the nation's educational system.

Family-Helping Organizations

Habitat for Humanity
121 Habitat Street
Americus, GA 31709-3498
912-924-6935
   This organization allows those who need a home to assist volunteers in building or rehabilitating the house they will live in.

Kids Hope USA
17011 Hickory
Spring Lake, MI 49456
616-846-7490
   This organization teaches neighborhood churches to link their congregations with at-risk elementary school students and their families.

Mothers At Home
8310-A Old Courthouse Road
Vienna, VA 22182
703-827-5903
   This organization supports mothers who choose to stay at home to nurture their families.

Project Intercept
P.O. Box 600307
San Diego, CA 92160-0307
619-271-0700
   This organization helps set up mentoring programs for at-risk youth.

The Urban Alternative
P.O. Box 4000
Dallas, TX 75208
214-943-3868
   This organization provides church-based solutions to urban problems in the areas of youth, job skills, male mentoring, business development, housing, health, education, and racial/cultural harmony.

Homosexuality

Crossover Ministries, Inc.
P.O. Box 23744
Lexington, KY 40523-3744
602-277-4941
   The main goal of this organization is to help people who are trying to leave the homosexual lifestyle. Crossover Ministries specializes in helping men who are struggling with transvestism and transsexualism.

Desert Stream
12488 Venice Blvd.
Los Angeles, CA 90066
310-572-0140

This organization helps people move out of the gay lifestyle. It offers counseling and educational information.

Genesis Counseling
307 East Chapman
Orange, CA 92666
714-744-3326

This organization provides speakers to represent the conservative view of homosexuality, gay-rights legislation, and human sexuality.

Literacy

Literacy Volunteers of America
5795 Widewaters
Syracuse, NY 13214
315-445-8000

This organization promotes literacy for all Americans by providing resources to encourage people to volunteer in their local areas to teach others to read.

National Right to Read Foundation
3220 N. Street NW, Suite 174
Washington, D.C. 20007
800-468-8911

This is a nonpartisan organization dedicated to the elimination of illiteracy by promoting phonics and values-based literature.

Reading Tree Productions
51 Arvesta Street
Springfield, MA 01118
413-782-5839
   This organization helps parents to instill a love for reading in their young children.

Parents' Rights

Institute for Justice
1001 Pennsylvania Ave. NW, Suite 200 South
Washington, D.C. 20004
202-457-4240
   This organization works to protect citizens' rights, including issues related to school choice and education.

Of the People
2111 Wilson Blvd., Suite 700
Arlington, VA 22201
703-351-5051
   This organization is working to have states adopt a Parents' Rights Amendment to their state constitutions.

American Center for Law and Justice
P.O. Box 64429
Virginia Beach, VA 23467
804-579-2489
   This is a public-interest law firm and educational group specializing in issues related to the family.

Rutherford Institute
P.O. Box 7482
Charlottesville, VA 22906-7482
804-978-3888
   The purpose of this non-profit legal and educational organization is to defend persons whose First Amendment religious liberties have been threatened.

Public Policy Organizations

Claremont Institute
250 West First Street, Suite 330
Claremont, CA 91711
909-621-6825

This organization is dedicated to restoring our nation's founding principles regarding economics, education, and foreign and domestic policy to the common mind of the American people.

Family Research Council
700 Thirteenth Street NW, Suite 500
Washington, D.C. 20005
202-393-2100

This organization is dedicated to defending the family and provides research on a variety of topics supporting pro-family policies.

Heritage Foundation
214 Massachusetts Ave. NE
Washington, D.C. 20002-4999
202-546-4400

This organization provides policy-makers with the data to craft sound conservative policies regarding economic, defense, foreign and domestic policy, and cultural issues.

Toward Tradition
P.O. Box 58
Mercer Island, WA 98040
206-236-3046

This conservative Jewish organization seeks to form a Judeo-Christian alliance in order to increase the influence of traditional morality in society.

Sex Education

Best Friends
2000 N Street NW, Suite 201
Washington, D.C. 20036
202-822-9266

This organization is an abstinence-based educational program for girls in grades 5 through 9 that fosters self-respect and promotes responsible behavior. It is headed by Elayne Bennett, wife of William Bennett.

An Educated Choice, Inc.
6201 Leesburg Pike, Suite 404
Falls Church, VA 22044
703-532-9459

A division of the National Association for Abstinence Education, this group is dedicated to teaching and promoting principles of chastity and self-discipline. Its junior and senior high school curriculum is entitled "Reasonable Reasons to Wait."

Sex and Family Education
1486 Montgomery Highway
Birmingham, AL 35216
205-979-0302

This organization educates teens about the physical and emotional consequences of premarital sex, motivating them to choose sexual abstinence until marriage. It also works to equip teens with the skills to control sexual desires and resist sexual pressures.

Teen-Aid
723 East Jackson
Spokane, WA 99207
509-482-2868

This organization provides resources to encourage abstinence as a premarital lifestyle. It publishes family-life curricula for junior and senior high schools, provides curricula on HIV, and conducts a parent seminar.

Notes

Chapter 1. The Public Orphanage

1. Steven Sample, quoted by the *San Diego Tribune* and cited in "Can Anyone Replace Families?" *Citizen*, 15 March 1993, 8.

2. "Putting Learning First: Governing and Managing the Schools for High Achievement," a statement by the Research and Policy Committee of the Committee for Economic Development, 477 Madison Avenue, New York, New York 10022, 1994, 4.

3. "A Profile of Parents of Eighth Graders," the National Center for Educational Statistics, cited in "Parental Involvement," *Education Week*, 18 November 1992, 3.

4. "The American Teacher Survey" sponsored by MetLife, P.O. Box 807, Madison Square Station, New York, N.Y. 10159-0807.

5. An excellent source on this is Gene Bedley's book, *The Big R: Responsibility* (Irvine, Calif.: People Wise Publications, 1985).

6. Alan Ehrenhalt, "Malaise and America's Schools," *Education Week*, 4 August 1993, 68.

7. Joel Spring, *The American School 1642–1985* (Whiteplains, N.Y.: Longman, 1986), 337.

Chapter 2. The New "Pro-Family" Movement

1. Brigitte Berger and Peter L. Berger, *The War Over the Family* (Garden City, N.Y.: Anchor Press/Doubleday, 1984), 63.

2. Leonard Kaplan, ed., *Education and the Family* (Needham Heights, Mass.: Allyn and Bacon, 1992), 308.

3. Tom Hess, "Panicked about your child's school?" *Citizen*, 16 January 1995, 10.

4. Mary E. Procidano and Celia B. Fisher, eds., *Contemporary Families: A Handbook for Professionals* (New York: Teachers College Press, 1992), 2.

5. James S. Coleman, "Family Involvement in Education," in *School, Family, and Community Interaction*, ed. Cheryl L. Fagnano and Beverly Z. Werber (Boulder, Colo.: Westview Press, 1994), 31.

6. Coleman, "Family Involvement," 36.

7. Glenn T. Stanton, "The Social Significance of the Traditional Two-Parent Family" (Colorado Springs: Focus on the Family Public Policy Division, January 1995), 3–4.

8. "Marriage and Divorce" as reported by the U.S. Census Bureau and cited in *Education Week*, 16 December 1992, 3.

9. George Gilder, *Wealth and Poverty* (New York: Basic Books, 1981), 16.

10. Stanton, "The Social Significance," 4.

11. Tina Trudel and Celia Fisher, "Dual-Wage Families," in *Contemporary Families*, 21.

12. Cindy I. Carlson, "Single-Parent Families," in *Contemporary Families*, 44.

13. James H. Bray and Sandra H. Berger, "Stepfamilies," in *Contemporary Families*, 70.

14. Gilder, *Wealth and Poverty*, 69.

15. Kaplan, *Education and the Family*, 16.

16. Berger and Berger, "Stepfamilies," 167.

Chapter 3. The School As Family

1. From "Kansas Quality Performance Accreditation: A Plan for Living, Learning and Working in a Global Society," Kansas State Board of Education, 12 March 1991.

2. Jacqueline P. Wiseman, *The Other Half: Wives of Alcoholics and Their Social-Psychological Situation* (New York, Aldine De Gruyter, 1991), 27.

3. Ibid., 130.

4. Jessica Portner, "Participation in School-Based Program Jumps 8.9 Percent," *Education Week*, 28 October 1992, 10.

5. Ibid., 10.

6. Ramona M. Asher, *Women With Alcoholic Husbands* (Chapel Hill, N.C.: The University of North Carolina Press, 1992), 150–151.

7. Michael Bauman, "The Dangerous Samaritans: How We Unintentionally Injure the Poor," *Imprimis*, January 1994, published by Hillsdale College, Hillsdale, Michigan 49242.

8. Warren Berger, "Is This the School of Tomorrow?" *Sesame Street Parents' Guide*, October 1993, 34–38.

9. Ibid., 38

10. Allan Carlson, "What Has Government Done to Our Families?" *Essays in Political Economy*, November 1991, 7, published by the Ludwig von Mises Institute, Auburn, Alabama.

11. Allan Carlson makes a powerful argument about this in his article "What Has Government Done to Our Families?"

12. John Silber, *Straight Shooting* (New York: Harper & Row, 1989), 29.

13. Spring, *The American School*, 324.

14. S. J. Ventua, S. M. Taffel, W. D. Mosher, and S. Henshaw, "Trends in Pregnancies and Pregnancy Rates, United States, 1980–1988," *Monthly Vital Statistics Report 41*, no. 6, supplement, published in 1992 by the National Center for Health Statistics, Hyattsville, Maryland.

15. Jessica Portner, "Little Change in Teenage Pregnancy Rate During the 80's Found," *Education Week*, 25 November 1992, 8.

16. Eric Buehrer, *The New Age Masquerade* (Brentwood, Tenn.: Wolgemuth and Hyatt, 1990), 98. This is a quotation from Mission SOAR, a program piloted in the Los Angeles public schools. It was removed due to parents' outrage. *The New Age Masquerade* is available for ten dollars from Gateways to Better Education, P.O. Box 514, Lake Forest, California 92630.

17. Debra Viandero, "Study Finds U.S. Schools Lag in Learning Attitudes," *Education Week*, 7 April 1993, 16. Viandero cites a study done by Richard Haynes and Donald A. Chalker of Western Carolina University that was presented at the 1993 annual meeting of the Association of Supervision and Curriculum Development.

18. LynNell Hancock, "Parents 'Crazy' for Federal Cash," *Newsweek*, 31 October 1994, 54–55.

19. William E. Davis, "Putting Learning First," *Education Week*, 7 December 1994, 37.

Chapter 4. Caring for the Whole Child

1. Deborah Cohen, "Gains Tied to Preschool Program Persist, Study Finds," *Education Week*, 5 May 1993, 5.

2. Ibid.

3. The Commission on Chapter 1, "Making Schools Work for Children in Poverty: A New Framework Prepared by the Commission on Chapter 1," 10 December 1992, as reported in *Education Week*, 13 January 1993, 46.

4. "The Progress of Nations," the United Nations Children's Fund, cited in "Children in Poverty," *Education Week*, 29 September 1993, 3.

5. Deborah Cohen, "New Study Links Lower I.Q. at Age 5 to Poverty," *Education Week*, 7 April 1993, 4.

6. Ibid.

7. Jessica Portner, "School Focus on Children's Mental Health Urged," *Education Week*, 23 June 1993, 14.

8. James R. Tompkins and Patricia L. Tompkins-McGill, *Surviving in Schools in the 1990's* (New York: University Press of America, 1993), 4.

9. Charles Leerhsen, "Helping Themselves," *Newsweek*, Summer 1991 special edition, 65.

10. Phyllis Schlafly, "Turning Schools into Psychiatrists' Couches," *Conservative Chronicle*, 31 October 1990, 20.

11. "Counselors to Help L.A. Students Deal with Issues Raised by Trials," *Education Week*, 3 March 1993, 4.

12. Jessica Portner, "Children's Advocates Seek to Influence Health-Care-Reform Plan," *Education Week*, 14 April 1993, 18.

13. "Nearly 10 Million Children Uninsured in 1992, Report Says," *Education Week*, 12 January 1994, 4.

14. The Commission on Chapter 1, "Making Schools Work," 47.

15. Portner, "Children's Advocates."

16. "Report Card Faults Nation on Children's Health Issues," *Education Week*, 13 October 1993.

17. Stanley M. Elam, et al., "The 25th Annual Phi Delta Kappan/Gallup Poll of the Public's Attitudes Toward the Public Schools," *Phi Delta Kappan*, October 1993, 137–52.

18. Ibid.

19. Ann Bradley, "Revamp Teacher Recruitment, Training, Continuing Education, Colleges Urged," *Education Week*, 2 December 1992.

20. Joanna Richardson, "New Curriculum Seeks to Update Principal Training," *Education Week*, 3 February 1993, 1.

21. Debra Viadero, "Minnesota Governor Advocates 'One Stop' Agency for Children," *Education Week*, 27 January 1993, 15.

22. Margaret Dunkle, "Putting People First Means Connecting Education to Other Services," *Education Week*, 3 March 1993, 44. Dunkle is the director of the Policy Exchange at the Institute for Educational Leadership.

23. Eric Miller, citing a statistic from the National Association of Working Women, *Future Vision* (Naperville, Ill.: Sourcebooks, Inc., 1991), 236.

24. Ibid.

25. Ibid., 44.

26. Portner, "School Focus," 16.

27. Deborah Cohen, "Stronger Links Between Schools and Child Care Sought," *Education Week*, 31 March 1993, 5.

28. Elam, "Phi Delta Kappan/Gallup Poll."

29. Cohen, "Stronger Links."

30. March Whitebook, director of the Child Care Employee Project, quoted by Deborah Cohen, "Low Wages, Turnover Still Hurt Child Care, Survey Finds," *Education Week*, 31 March 1993, 5.

31. Deborah Cohen, "Focus On Quality and Availability of Child Care Urged," *Education Week*, 24 March 1993, 1.

32. Deborah Cohen, "Perry Preschool Graduates Show Dramatic New Social Gains at 27," *Education Week*, 21 April 1993, 1.

33. Deborah Cohen, "Head Start Faces a New Round of Political Scrutiny," *Education Week*, 31 March 1993, 1.

34. Howard Richman, "Re-Examining Head Start," *Education Week*, 21 October 1992, 32.

35. Cohen, "Head Start."

36. Cohen, "Stronger Links."

Chapter 5. Troubles in the Orphanage

1. Millicent Lawton, "Teenage Males Said More Apt to Die from Gunshots Than Natural Causes," *Education Week*, 20 March 1991, 3.

2. "Teenage Firearm Death Rate Leaps 77 percent in Five Years, Study Finds," *Education Week*, 31 March 1993, 2.

3. The Center to Prevent Handgun Violence, quoted in "Roll Call of the Dead," *People Weekly*, 14 June 1993, 50.

4. Jon D. Hull, "The Knife in the Book Bag," *Time*, 8 February 1993, 37.

5. Susan Reed, "Reading, Writing, and Murder," *People Weekly*, 4 June 1993, 44.

6. "Student in Mass. High School Fatally Stabbed During Class," *Education Week*, 21 April 1993, 2.

7. "Kids Count Data Book," Center for the Study of Social Policy, 1250 I St., N.W., Suite 503, Washington, D.C. 20005.

8. Millicent Lawton, "'Anywhere, At Any Time' Violence in Schools Spreads Past Cities," *Education Week*, 5 May 1993, 1.

9. Jessica Portner, "School Violence Up Over Past 5 Years, 82 percent in Survey Say," *Education Week*, 12 January 1994, 9.

10. The Ravenswood City Elementary School District of East Palo Alto, California considered providing life insurance which included the cost of burial service for low-income families. As reported by Millicent Lawton, "Violence-Ridden District Weighing Burial Insurance for Students," *Education Week*, 27 January 1993, 8.

11. *Education Week*, 23 June 1993, 3, and 14 July 1993, 3.

12. "Teacher Victimization," *Education Week*, 7 April 1993, 7.

13. Jon D. Hull, "The Knife in the Book Bag," 37, and *Education Week*, 3 February 1993, 2, and 21 April 1993, 3.

14. "Teacher Victimization," *Education Week*, 7 April 1994, 7. One percent of rural teachers reported being attacked making the average of violence against all teachers approximately 2.5 percent nationwide.

15. Jessica Portner, "School Violence Up Over Past 5 Years."

16. "Youth Violence: Gangs on Main Street, U.S.A.," Pew Partnership for Civic Change, 145-C Ednam Dr., Charlottesville, Virginia 22903. Copies of this report can be obtained for two dollars.

17. *Education Week*, 17 February 1993, 2.

18. *Education Week*, 19 May 1993, 3

19. *Education Week*, 26 January 1994, 4.

20. "Babes with arms," *American School Board Journal*, November 1994, 6.

21. Eric Buehrer, *Creating A Positive Public School Experience* (Nashville: Thomas Nelson, 1994), 135.

22. Sara Sklaroff, "Drug Use Among High Schoolers Up After Period of Decline, Study Finds," *Education Week*, 9 February 1994, 8.

23. Jessica Portner, "8th Graders' Use of Drugs on the Rise, Survey Finds," *Education Week*, 21 April 1993, 12.

24. *Education Week*, 22 September 1993, 2.

25. Jessica Portner, "Efforts to Curb Teenage Drinking Said to Fall Short," *Education Week*, 5 May 1993, 11.

26. Portner, "Efforts to Curb Teenage Drinking Said to Fall Short," compared with Portner's article, "Safety Board Urges Crackdown on Teenage Drunken Driving."

27. Michael Josephson, *Ethical Values, Attitudes, and Behaviors in American Schools* (Marina del Ray, Calif.: Josepheson Institute of Ethics, 1992), 23.

28. "Single-Parent Families," *Education Week*, 19 June 1991.

29. Miller, *Future Vision*, 42.

30. Ibid.

31. Peter Schmidt, "Neighborhood Impact on Boys' Dropout Rates Seen Limited," *Education Week*, 13 January 1993, 9, reporting on a study done by the Urban Institute, "The Effect of Neighborhood Characteristics on Dropping Out Among Teenage Boys." For a copy call 202-833-7200.

32. "When Households Continue, Discontinue, and Form," Series P-23, no. 179 (Washington, D.C.: Superintendent of Documents, U.S. Government Printing Office), cited in Deborah Cohen, "Family Breakup and Income Are Linked Census Data Reveal," *Education Week*, 27 January 1993, 1.

33. *Journal of the American Medical Association*, 15 September 1993, cited in Deborah Cohen, "Frequent Moves Said to Boost Risk of School Problems," *Education Week*, 22 September 1993, 15.

34. "Student Mobility," *Education Week*, 23 June 1993, 7, as reported by the National Center for Education Statistics.

35. Deborah Cohen, "Stress in Balancing Work and Family More Likely Felt at Home, Study Finds," *Education Week*, 15 September 1993, 10 (reporting on a study done by the Families and Work Institute, 212-465-2044).

36. Miller, *Future Vision*, 238.

37. Ibid.,201.

38. Anh Do, "Pupils Learn Lessons For After-School Life," *The Orange County Register*, March 28, 1993, B-1.

39. Jessica Portner, "Efforts to Curb Teenage Drinking," 11.

40. Jessica Portner, "Prevention Efforts in Junior High Found Not to Curb Drug Use in High School," *Education Week*, 16 June 1993, 9 (reporting on "Preventing Adolescent Drug Use: Long-Term Results of a Junior High Program").

41. Sylvester Monroe, "D.A.R.E. Bedeviled," *Time*, 17 October 1994, 49.

42. Eric Miller, *Future Vision*, 177.

43. William Strein, "Classroom-Based Elementary School Affective Education Programs: A Critical Review," *Psychology in the Schools* 25 (1988): 288–96.

44. William Strein, 294.

45. *Preventive Medicine* 17, 145, as reported by Rick Branch in "Affective Education: A Statistical Analysis," *Watchman Expositor* 9, no. 5 (1992): 3.

46. Ibid., 135.

47. Michael Josephson, *Ethical Values*, 3.

48. Ibid., 19.

49. Ibid., 21–22.

50. Fred Schab, "Schooling Without Learning: Thirty Years of Cheating in High School," *Adolescence* 26 (Winter 1991): 104.

51. Josephson, *Ethical Values*, 71.

52. "Arkansas High Court Upholds Listing of Principal Who Paddled Student," *Education Week*, 17 March 1993, 2.

53. *Education Week*, 3 November 1993, 3.

54. "Arizona Board Reverses Stand On School Corporal Punishment," *Education Week*, 10 February 1993, 2.

55. "Parental Discipline," *Education Week*, May 19, 1993, 3 (Reporting the findings of Bruskin/Goldring Research, 100 Metroplex Dr., Edison, New Jersey 08817).

56. Debra Viadero, "Election Talk Aside, Education in Values Gains Momentum," *Education Week*, 21 October 1992, 12.

57. Tom Minnery, "High-Tech Follies," *Focus On The Family Citizen*, 21 February 1994, 5.

58. Jessica Portner, "Fightings War on Weapons," *Education Week*, 8 December 1993, 24.

59. Millicent Lawton, "Program Found Curbing Children's Violent Behavior," *Education Week*, 5 May 1993, 14.

60. Donna Harrington-Lueker, "Hanging on to Hope," *The American School Board Journal*, December 1994, 18.

61. Ibid.

Chapter 6. From Schools to Orphanages: A Quick History

1. Joel Spring, *The American School 1642-1985*, 1, 28.

2. Ibid., 28.

3. Thomas Jefferson, "To Edward Carrington," in Gordon Lee, ed., *Crusade Against Ignorance: Thomas Jefferson on Education* (New York: Teachers College Press, 1961), 102, cited by Spring, *The American School*, 40.

4. Henry Perkinson, *The Imperfect Panacea: American Faith in Education 1865–1965* (New York: Random House, 1968), 9.

5. John Gatto in a foreword to Cathy Duffy, *Government Nannies* (Gresham, Ore.: Noble Publishing Associates, 1995), xi.

6. Wayne E. Fuller, *The Old Country School* (Chicago: University of Chicago, 1982), 34.

7. Perkinson, *The Imperfect Panacea*, 11.

8. David R. Reynolds and Fred M. Shelley, "Local Control in American Public Education: Myth and Reality," in *Geographic Dimensions of United States Social Policy*, ed. Janet Kondras and John Paul Jones III (London: Edward Arnold Publishing, 1990), 112–13.

9. Spring, *The American School*, 84.

10. Reynolds and Shelley, "Local Control," 113.

11. Ibid., 113. For further exploration on this point see Ruth Elson, *Guardians of Tradition* (Lincoln: University of Nebraska, 1964), 208–11, 289–90.

12. Spring, *The American School*, 71.

13. George Smith, "Nineteenth-Century Opponents of State Education: Prophets of Modern Revisionsim," chapter 3 in *The Public School Monopoly*, ed. Robert Everhart (Cambridge, Mass.: Ballinger, 1982),112.

14. Ibid., 128.

15. Reynolds and Shelley, "Local Control," 113.

16. Ibid., 115.

17. Perkinson, *The Imperfect Panacea*, 70.

18. Spring, *The American School*, 73.

19. Reynolds and Shelley, "Local Control," 118.

20. Perkinson, *The Imperfect Panacea*, 71.

21. Spring, *The American School*, 227.

22. Reynolds and Shelley, "Local Control," 122.

23. Spring, *The American School*, 295.

24. Ibid., 308.

25. Ibid., 19-20.

26. Ibid., 34.

Chapter 7. Clashes Over Selection of Materials

1. "Parents Protest Book," *American School Board Journal*, December 1993, 5.

2. Steve Garnass, "Principal to replace banned books," *Denver Post*, 5 March 1994.

3. Phyllis Schlafly, "Who Are the Real Censors?" *The Phyllis Schlafly Report*, August 1990.

4. "The Top Ten Banned Books," *The New York Times*, 13 October 1993. The other books and curricula listed included: *Pumsy in Pursuit of Excellence, Developing Understanding of Self and Others, Quest, The Bridge to Terabithia, The Catcher in the Rye, The Boy Who Lost His Face*, and *Of Mice and Men*.

5. Schlafly, "Who Are The Real Censors?".

6. Ibid.

7. "In The Beginning," a chart in *U.S. News & World Report*, 23 December 1991, 59.

8. Benjamin Sendor, "What's a Pamphlet or 10 Among Friends?" *The American School Board Journal*, March 1994, 14.

9. Dave Condren, "Book Controversy in Colden Settled," *The Buffalo News*, 20 January 1994, A1.

10. Jill Carlson, *What Are Your Kids Reading?* (Nashville: Wolgemuth & Hyatt, 1991), 4.

11. Ibid., 62.

12. Ann Bradley, "Christian Activists Score Gains in San Diego County," *Education Week*, 18 November 1992, 12.

13. Debra Viadero, "Civil-Liberties Group Seeks to Contest Conservative Activists," *Education Week*, 10 March 1993, 18.

14. Meg Sommerfeld, "Christian Activists Seek to Torpedo NASDC Project," *Education Week*, 10 March 1993, 1.

15. Jessica Portner, "Georgia Panel Proposes Broadening Teaching about Sex," *Education Week*, 4 November 1992, 31.

16. "Virginia Outcomes-Based Program Abandoned by State Board," *Education Week*, 13 November 1993.

17. Vincent Carroll, "In Littleton, Colorado, Voters Expel Education Faddists," *The Wall Street Journal*, 18 November 1993.

18. William J. Bennett, "The War Over Culture in Education," *The Heritage Lectures #341* (Washington, D.C.: The Heritage Foundation, 1991).

19. "Teacher Education for the Twenty-First Century," *American Association of State Colleges and Universities*, 1992.

20. "Work and Family Life," Ohio's Competency Analysis Profile, 1992, published by the Vocational Instructional Materials Laboratory, Ohio State University, 1900 Kenny Road, Columbus, Ohio 43210-1090.

21. "Testing Assumptions: A Survey of Teachers' Attitudes Toward the Nation's Reform Agenda," published by LH Research, 1270 Avenue of the Americas, Suite 2308, New York, New York 10020, cited in "Teachers Question Reform Agenda," *Teachers Magazine*, November/December 1993, 13.

22. Jennifer Chauhan, "Just a Phone Call Away," *Teachers Magazine*, February 1994, 16–17.

23. Jill Carlson, *Defending the Freedom to Learn*, self-published, 1992, 15. (This booklet can be ordered for four dollars by writing to Jill Carlson, 1527 South Union, Cedar Falls, Iowa 50613).

24. Ibid., 18.

25. Peter Brimelow and Leslie Spencer, "The National Extortion Association?" *Forbes*, 7 June 1993.

26. "A Matter of Choice," *Education Week*, special-report insert, 16 December 1992.

27. Brimelow and Spencer, "The National Extortion Association?"

28. Ann Bradely, "Merger Creates New International Teachers' Group," *Education Week*, 3 February 1993, 14.

29. Ibid.

30. "NEA Disrespect for Home and Parents," *The Phyllis Schlafly Report*, August 1991, refering to resolution C-39.

31. From a 10 July 1991 press release by California Common Cause NEWS, 1535 Mission Street, San Francisco, California 94103.

32. "Before Census, NEA Laid Groundwork," *Education Week*, 28 October 1992, 16.

33. Ibid.

34. Berry Morson, "Teacher Union Link to Liberals Irks Candidates," *Rocky Mountain News*, 10 October 1993.

35. *Education Week*, 17 March 1993, 22.

36. "The American Teacher Survey," MetLife, P.O. Box 807, Madison Square Station, New York, New York 10159-0807.

Chapter 8. Sex Education and School Clinics

1. Nina Darnton, "The End of Innocence," *Newsweek*, Special Issue, 1993, 62–64.

2. Charles Sykes, *A Nation of Victims* (New York: St. Martin's, 1992), 246.

3. "SIECUS Report Faults Gaps in Sex-Education Curricula," *Education Week*, 20 October 1993.

4. Barbara Dafoe Whitehead, "The Failure of Sex Education," *The Atlantic Monthly*, October 1994, 64.

5. Joy G. Dryfoos, *Full-Service Schools* (San Francisco: Jossey-Bass Publishers, 1994), 5.

6. Ibid., 12.

7. Susan Larson, "Do School-Based Clinics Work?" *Family Policy* 1, no. 4 (published by Family Research Council, Washington, D.C., March 1991): 1.

8. Dryfoos, *Full-Service Schools*, 15.

9. Ibid., 16.

10. Ibid., 84.

11. Elam, "Phi Delta Kappan/Gallup Poll", 137–52.

12. Dryfoos, *Full-Service Schools*, 9.

13. Stan E. Weed and Joseph A. Olsen, "Effects of Family Planning Programs for Teenagers of Adolescent Birth and Pregnancy Rates," *Family Planning Perspectives*, 20, no. 3 (1985): 153, as reported in Susan Larson, "Do School-Based Clinics Work?" 3.

14. Jessica Portner, "Book Examines Debate Over Condoms in Schools," *Education Week*, 21 April 1993, 13.

15. Whitehead, "The Failure of Sex Education," 70.

16. Ibid., 72.

17. From a news report in the Health Section of *Education Week*, 23 June 1993, 14.

18. David Ruenzel, "Going Too Far," *Teacher Magazine*, November/December 1993, 26.

19. "Let's Talk About Sexuality: Opening Doors for Parents and Kids," published by the Washington Alliance Concerned with School-Age Parents, 2366 Eastlake Ave. E., Suite 408, Seattle, Washington 98102, 1990.

20. State laws like California Penal Code section 647.6 deal with such activity. Detective W. E. Davis of the La Palma, California, Police Department comments that, "Such laws are designed, in part, to protect children from things such as being told sexually explicit information from an adult who, for instance, they may meet in a park. Young children might not always feel annoyed by such adult talk but that doesn't mean the law would not be applied for their protection." Charges of obscenity take into account reasonable community standards and prohibit material that is not artistic, literary, or scientific in nature. One has to ask the artistic, literary, or scientific merits of certain sex-education courses.

21. Ruenzel, "Going Too Far," 25.

22. Ibid.

23. Suzanne Alexander, "New Grade-School Sexuality Classes Go Beyond Birds and Bees to Explicit Basics," *The Wall Street Journal*, 2 April 1993.

24. Ruenzel, "Going Too Far," 25.

25. Andy Gabron and Steve Kaminski, "Out of Control," *Focus on the Family Citizen*, 21 February 1994, 6.

26. Alexander, "New Grade-School Sexuality Classes."

27. *Education Week*, 5 May 1993, 3.

28. Suzanne Fields, "Children Have No Moral Compass," *Conservative Chronicle*, 1993.

29. "They Didn't Laugh," *Teacher Magazine*, November/December 1993, 12.

30. Alexander, "New Grade-School Sexuality Classes."

Chapter 9. Feminism and the Classroom

1. Myron Lieberman, *Public Education: An Autopsy* (Cambridge, Mass.: Harvard University, 1993), 32.

2. Charles J. Sykes, *A Nation of Victims* (New York: St. Martin's, 1992), 180.

3. Allan C. Carlson, *From Cottage to Workstation* (San Francisco: Ignatius Press, 1993), 61–62.

4. "ACLU Alleges Gender Bias in Test for Merit Scholarships," *Education Week*, 23 February 1994, 4.

5. C. A. Bowers and David Flinders, *Culturally Responsive Teaching and Supervision* (New York: Teachers College Press, 1991), 21.

6. Millicent Lawton, "Girls Will and Should be Girls," *Education Week*, 30 March 1994, 24–27.

7. Ibid.

8. Amy Saltzman, "Schooled in failure?" *U.S. News & World Report*, 7 November 1994, 88–93.

9. Eugene H. Owen, comp., "Trends in Academic Progress: Achievement of American Students in Science, 1970–90, Mathematics, 1973–90, Reading, 1971–90, and Writing, 1984–90" (Washington, D.C.: the National Center for Educational Statistics, U.S. Department of Education), 26–27.

10. Boys dropped from an average score of 314 to 292; girls dropped from 297 to 275 ("Trends in Academic Progress," 24).

11. Ibid., 25.

12. Paul C. Vitz, *Censorship: Evidence of Bias in Our Children's Textbooks* (Ann Arbor, Mich.: Servant, 1986), 41.

13. Ibid., 42.

14. Ibid., 73.

15. Ibid., 75.

16. Nan Stein, "School Harassment—An Update," *Education Week*, 4 November 1992, 37.

17. Amy Saltzman, "It's not just teasing," *U.S. News & World Report*, 6 December 1993, 73–77.

18. Charles Sykes, in his book *A Nation of Victims*, reports that the Association of American Colleges' Project on the Status of Women includes men's domination of classroom discussions as sexual harassment (page 189).

19. Mark Walsh, "OCR Urges 'Forceful' Reaction to Harassment of Children," *Education Week*, 12 May 1993, 5.

20. Amy Saltzman, "It's not just teasing."

21. Ibid.

22. Lieberman, *Public Education: An Autopsy*, 26.

Chapter 10. The New Liberal Arts 101: Multiculturalism

1. Lieberman, *Public Education: An Autopsy*, 38.

2. Thomas Sowell, *Inside American Education* (New York: The Free Press, 1993), 225.

3. Peter Schmidt, "Study Finds Immigrants' Children Face Some Risks in Assimilating," *Education Week*, 4 August 1993, 14.

4. "Language Spoken at Home and Ability to Speak English for United States, Regions and States: 1990," report number CPH-L-133 (Washington, D.C.: Population Division, Statistical Information Office, Census Bureau, 1990).

5. Peter Schmidt, "Asian School-Age Population Expected to Double by 2020," *Education Week*, 24 February 1993, 5.

6. "Improve Teacher-Training to Help Meet Hispanic Students' Needs, Report Urges," *Education Week*, 3 November 1993, 13.

7. Jay Taylor, "Immigration," Education Vital Signs, The American School Board Journal, December 1993, A-8.

8. Peter Schmidt, "Desegregation Study Spurs Debate Over Equity Remedies," *Education Week*, 12 January 1994, 5.

9. Peter Schmidt, "Symposium Urges Youth Agencies to Be 'Hip' to City Teenagers," *Education Week*, 10 March 1993, 5.

10. Ibid.

11. Peter Schmidt, "Anthropologist's Study of Capital High School Reveals the Roots of Blacks' Underachievement," *Education Week*, 9 June 1993, 6–7.

12. Rod Janzen, "Melting Pot or Mosaic?" *Educational Leadership* 51, no. 8 (May 1994): 9–11.

13. James Banks, "Transforming the Mainstream Curriculum," *Educational Leadership* 51, no. 8 (May 1994): 4–8.

14. Ibid.

15. Banks, "Transforming the Mainstream Curriculum," 4.

16. Peter West, "Academy Unveils 'Principles' for Science Standards," *Education Week*, 4 November 1992, 10.

17. Bill Bigelow, "Once Upon a Quincentenary," *Radical Teacher*, no. 44 (Winter 1993): 7.

18. Ibid., 6.

19. Ibid., 1.

20. Johanna Richardson, "Shattering Stereotypes, Education School Seeks to 'Serve Needs of Diverse Learner,'" *Education Week*, 7 April 1993, 6.

21. Paul Harvey, "If our Ancestors Had Stayed Put," *Los Angeles Times Syndicate*, 1993.

22. "Wisconsin Attorney General Says School Indian Nicknames May Violate Law," *Education Week*, 28 October 1992, 2.

23. Louise Dermon-Sparks and the ABC Task Force, Anti-Bias Curriculum: Tools for Empowering Young Children (Washington, D.C.: National Association for the Education of Young Children, 1989), 90–91.

24. Ibid., 88–89.

25. Ibid., 91–93.

26. "Voters Say No to 'America First,'" *The American School Board Journal*, November 1994, 16–17.

Chapter 11. The New Liberal Arts 102: Eco-Educators and Global Educators

1. Worksheet called "Indian Trail Activity" from the outdoor education program at Camp Waskowitz.

2. "A Scare Tactic," *Education Week*, 28 October 1992, 2.

3. Peter West, "Skeptics Questioning the Accuracy, Bias of Environmental Education," *Education Week*, 16 June 1993, 1.

4. Miller, *Future Vision*, 211.

5. Ibid., 223.

6. Kenneth A. Tye, ed., *Global Education: School-based Strategies* (Orange, Calif.: Interdependence Press, 1990), 132.

7. Ibid., 28.

8. Ibid., 47.

9. Ibid.

10. Tye, *Global Education*, 57.

11. Ibid., 59.

12. Ibid., 137.

13. Buehrer, *The New Age Masquerade*, 143, quoting Gregg Cunningham's U.S. Department of Education's analysis of the Center for Teaching International Relations' "World Citizen Curriculum."

14. Philip Vander Velde and Hyung-Chan Kim, eds., *Global Mandate: Pedagogy for Peace* (Bellingham, Wash.: Bellwether Press, 1985), 352–53.

15. Jessica Portner, "Aiming to Put 'Peace Literacy' into Curricula, Columnist Launches a Course on Nonviolence," *Education Week*, 18 November 1992, 6.

16. Tye, Global Education, 60.

17. Ibid., 62.

Chapter 12. The Gay Nineties: Homosexuality in the Classroom

1. From a press release issued by the Los Angeles Unified School District Gay and Lesbian Education Commission, Kathy Gill, director.

2. David Greenberg, *The Construction of Homosexuality* (Chicago: University of Chicago, 1988), 454.

3. Ibid.

4. Ibid., 460.

5. Ibid., referring to an annual poll conducted by UCLA and the American Council of Education surveying 180,000 students attending 345 schools.

6. Ibid., 462.

7. Ibid.

8. Ibid., 463.

9. Jessica Portner, "Florida School's Health Fair Offers Free Tests for AIDS Virus," *Education Week*, 15 December 1993, 5.

10. From *Education Week*, 9 June 1993, 12, citing the San Francisco Department of Health report "Youth and HIV Disease in San Franciso," conducted in 1992 and 1993.

11. "Problems Facing Gays and Lesbians," a flyer produced by the Los Angeles Unified School District Gay and Lesbian Education Commission.

12. Kathy Gill, "A Call for Human Rights," GLEC Los Angeles (Gay and Lesbian Education Commission of Los Angeles), Summer 1994, 7.

13. Resolution passed by the Colorado PTA Board of Directors 11 February 1994. The resolution was handily defeated at the state convention.

14. Millicent Lawton, "Mass. Report Calls for Policies to Aid Gay Students," *Education Week*, 10 March 1993, 20.

15. Beth Rens, "Why Should the Public Schools Teach about Sexual Orientation?" a paper presented to the annual meeting of the Association for Sexuality Education and Training, 22 September 1989, 2. Rens is a public health educator for the Seattle-King County Department of Public Health.

16. Peter LaBarbera, "Gay Youth Suicide: Myth Is Used to Promote Homosexual Agenda," *Insight*, published by the Family Research Council, 700 Thirteenth Street NW, Suite 500, Washington, D.C. 20005, 1.

17. Ibid., 3.

18. Ibid., 5.

19. Ibid., 6, citing a letter Susan Blumenthal wrote to the *Journal of the American Medical Association*, 5 June 1991, 2806–7.

20. Ibid., 7.

21. From a brochure promoting the video Gay Youth, produced by Bay Area Network of Gay and Lesbian Educators. In a telephone interview the distributer told me the video is "selling well" and being distributed to public schools "every week."

22. Marshall Kirk and Hunter Madsen, *After the Ball: How America Will Conquer Its Fear and Hatred of Gays in the 1990s* (New York: Doubleday, 1990), 183, quoted by LaBarbera, "Gay Youth Suicide," 10.

23. NEA resolution C-30, "Family Life Education," passed in 1990.

24. From the brochure for the event "A Woman's Place Is in the Curriculum," 22–23 September and 1 November 1989.

25. Interview with Eadie Gieb, director of Parents and Students United of the San Fernando Valley, 14 June 1994.

26. From a 1993 flyer distributed by the Homecoming Project, 77 South Main Street, Seattle, Washington 98104.

27. M. Consdidine and E. Reis, *High Risk—High Return: Talking to Teens about Sexuality in the 90s*, Appendix G: Teacher's Glossary.

28. Rens, "Why Should the Public Schools Teach About Sexual Orientation?"

29. From a handout entitled "Recommendations for Public Schools" from the Institute for Sexual Inclusiveness through Training and Education (INSITE).

30. From a flyer entitled "Strategies for Teachers" published by the Institute for Sexual Inclusiveness through Training and Education (INSITE).

31. Adam Behrman and Jane Futcher, Building Bridges: *Exploring the Needs of the Lesbian and Gay Community*, Inservice Training Guide, United Way of the Bay Area Member and Grant Agencies, Fall, 1990, p. 48.

Chapter 13. Pedophilia: The Next Civil Right?

1. Lester Kirkendall, "Sex Education in the Future," *Journal of Sex Education and Therapy*, Spring/Summer 1985, quoted by J. A. Reisman and E. W. Eichel in *Kinsey: Sex and Fraud* (Lafayette, La.: 1990: Lochinvar-Huntington House), 131.

2. David Thorstad, "Man/Boy Love and the American Gay Movement," *Journal of Homosexuality* 20, no. 1/2, : 253.

3. Ibid., 269.

4. Ibid., 257.

5. Ibid., 257–258.

6. Michael Ebert, "Pedophilia Steps into the Daylight," *Citizen* magazine, 16 November 1992, 7.

7. John Leo, "Cradle-to-Grave Intimacy," *Time*, 7 September 1981, 69.

8. Ebert, "Pedophilia," 6.

9. Ibid., 7.

10. Joseph Geraci and Donald Mader, "Interview: John Money," *Paidika* (Amsterdam, The Netherlands: Spring 1991), 5.

11. Ibid., 12.

12. Leo, "Cradle-to-Grave Intimacy."

13. Ibid.

14. Gerald Jones, "The Study of Intergenerational Intimacy in North America: Beyond Politics and Pedophila," *Journal of Homosexuality* 280.

15. "Statement of Purpose," *Paidika*, (Amsterdam, The Netherlands: Summer 1987).

16. Geraci and Mader, "Interview: John Money, " 5. The authors refer to a previous statement by Dr. Money.

17. Theo Sandfort, Edward Brongersma, and Alex van Naerssen, "Man-Boy Relationships: Different Concepts for a Diversity of Phenomena," *Journal of Homosexuality*, 1991, 20, no. 1/2) : 10.

18. Chin-Keung Li, "'The Main Thing Is Being Wanted': Some Case Studies on Adult Sexual Experiences with Children," *Journal of Homosexuality*, 1991, 20, no. 1/2, 133.

19. Ken Plummer, "Understanding Childhood Sexualities," *Journal of Homosexuality*, 1991, 20, no. 1/2, 241.

20. Geraci and Mader, "Interview: John Money," 13.

21. Ibid., 9.

22. Sandfort, Brongersma, and van Naerssen, "Man-Boy Relationships," 10.

23. Chin-Keung Li, "'The Main Thing,'" 136.

24. Peter Schmidt, "Teacher's Advocacy of Pedophilia Raises Legal Questions," Education Week, 1 December 1993, 3.

Chapter 14. The Value of Learning in the Orphanage

1. Ann Bradley, "Not Making The Grade," *Education Week*, 15 September, 1993, 19.

2. Ibid., 1.

3. Freda Schwartz, "Statistics: The Treacherous Task-Master," *Education Week*, 18 November 1992, 27.

4. Alston Chase, "In the Classroom, We Have Lost the Work Ethic," *Orange County Register*, 15 May 1991, K3.

5. Debra Viadero, "Study Finds U.S. Schools Lag in Learning Attitudes," *Education Week*, 7 April 1993, 16.

6. Owen, comp., "Trends in Academic Progress," 19.

7. "The Condition of Education 1994" (Washington, D.C.: U.S. Department of Education, August 1994) 212.

8. Ibid., 206–7.

9. Owen, "Trends in Academic Progress," 1–19.

10. "The Condition of Education 1992" (Washington, D.C.: U.S. Department of Education, June 1992), 44.

11. Owen, "Trends in Academic Progress," 21–23.

12. Merle Marsh, "12 Difficulties Encountered When Attempting to Start a Revolution in Education," *Education Week*, 25 November 1992, 20.

13. James Steffensen, "Can We Make Light Bulbs from Candles?" *Education Week*, 2 December 1992, 28.

14. Douglas Carnine, "Facts Over Fads," *Education Week*, 8 December 1993, 40.

15. Joe Nathan, "Alice in Reformland," *Education Week*, 17 February 1993, 36.

16. Carnine, "Facts Over Fads," 40.

17. "Will New Math Add Up to Plus for Schoolkids?" *Los Angeles Times*, 12 March 1995, A3.

18. "An Academic Shift," *Teacher Magazine*, February 1994, 8.

19. David Angus and Jeffrey Mirel, "High School Course-Taking and Educational Reform," *Education Week*, 17 November 1993.

20. Perry A. Zirkel, "Grade Inflation: A Problem and a Proposal," *Education Week*, 8 March 1995, 28. Refer also to statistics outlined in *Education Week*, 15 January 1995.

21. William Spady, "Transforming Schools for the 21st Century," general-session materials presented at a seminar in Anaheim, California, April 28–May 1, 1994, conducted by the High Success Network, 17.

22. Ibid, 200.

23. Interview with William Spady, 2 November 1994.

24. Ibid.

25. Ibid.

26. "Outcome Based Education Comes Under Attack," The Association of Supervision and Curriculum Development's *Update* 36, no. 3 (March 1994): 4.

27. Albert Shanker, "Outrageous Outcomes," *The New York Times*, 12 September 1993, E7.

28. Ibid.

29. Steven Kossor, "The Psychological Abuses of OBE," *Free World Research Report* 3, no. 8 (August 1994): 1.

30. From a telephone interview with a parent in New York.

31. From a telephone interview with a parent in Michigan, 15 March 1994.

32. Judith Anderson, "Who's in Charge? Teachers' Views on Control Over School Policy and Classroom Practices," *Education Research Report*, published by the Office of Educational Research and Improvement of the U. S. Department of Education, August 1994.

33. "Global Activities: Teaching Ideas for K-12 Educators," Co-sponsored and developed by The Iowa Department of Education, Iowa Area Education Agencies, et al, printed by the Dubuque Community School District, 63.

Chapter 15. The Feds Are Coming!

1. *Goals 2000: Educate America Act*, Public Law 103-227, I, 102.

2. Gilder, *Wealth and Poverty*, 112.

3. Ibid.

4. *Goals 2000: Educate America Act*, III, 301 (7).

5. *The National Education Goals Report*, vol. 1, 1993, U.S. Department of Education, 45.

6. Debra Viadero, "Making the Grade," *Teacher Magazine*, March 1995, 19.

7. *The National Education Goals Report*, 68.

8. Ibid., 66.

9. For a complete analysis of this issue refer to Cathy Duffy's book, *Government Nannies* (Gresham, Ore.: Noble, 1995).

10. *Goals 2000: Educate America Act*, I, 10, 102 (4)(B)(i).

11. Rita Kramer, *Ed School Follies* (New York: Free Press, 1991), 82.

12. Ibid., 19.

13. "Reaching Out: Building Bridges to a Better World," the program of the conference of the California Association for the Education of Young Children, 10–12 March 1995.

14. Kramer, *Ed School Follies*, 15.

15. William Bennett, *The De-Valuing of America* (New York: Touchstone, 1992,) 53.

16. Judd Gregg, "A Federal Grab for Control of Schools," *The Washington Times*, 31 January 1994.

17. Lynne V. Chenney, "The End of History," *Wall Street Journal*, 20 October 1994; and a newsletter from Gary Bauer of the Family Research Council, 3 February 1995.

18. *Goals 2000: Educate America Act*, 213(a)(2)(ii).

19. Ibid., 213(a)(2)(iv).

20. Judd Gregg, "A Federal Grab for Control of Schools."

21. Margaret Wang, Maynard Reynolds, and Herbert Walberg, "Reform All Categorical Programs," *Education Week*, 24 March 1993, 64.

22. Telephone interview with Tom Fagan of the Goals 2000 office within the U.S. Department of Education, 5 October 1994.

23. *Goals 2000: Educate America Act*, Section 213,(f)(1)(C)(ii).

24. Ibid., Section 220(c)(2).

25. Ibid., Section 213, (c)(2)(A)-(G).

26. Ibid., Section 306, (f)(2).

27. John Hood, "Education: Is America Spending Too Much?" Cato Policy Analysis, no. 126 (18 January 1990) 10–11, cited by William F. Lauber, "Goals 2000: The 'Washington Knows Best' Approach to School Reform," The Heritage Foundation's Issue Bulletin, no. 185 (16 November 1993): 5.

28. Tommy M. Tomlinson, "Class Size and Public Policy: Politics and Panaceas" (Washington, D.C.: U.S. Department of Education: Office of Educational Research and Improvement, 1988), 1.

29. Lauber, "Goals 2000," in Heritage Foundation Issue Bulletin no. 185, 7.

30. Eric Hanushek, *Making Schools Work* (Washington, D.C.: The Brookings Institute, 1994), 64.

31. *60 Minutes*, 27 February 1994.

32. Ibid.

33. Ibid.

Chapter 16. Encouraging Signs

1. Trinh T. Le, "Educator stresses philosophy," *Port Arthur News*, 7 November 1992.

2. Hope E. Paasch, "Making the grade," *Houston Post*, 4 November 1988, A1.

3. Kimberly Easlely, "Inefficient teachers should 'hit the door,'" *Huntsville Item*, 25 June 1992, 1.

4. Thaddeus Lott, "One school's fight should be everyone's battle," *Houston Chronicle*, 23 June 1991, E1.

5. David Kaplan, "The elementary success of Thaddeus Lott," *Houston Post*, 23 February 1992, E6.

6. George Seldes, *The Great Thoughts* (New York: Ballantine, 1985), 382.

7. Larry Cuban, "A National Curriculum and Tests: Charting the Direct and Indirect Consequences," *Education Week*, 14 July 1993, 25.

8. William Bennet, *The De-Valuing of America*, 77–78.

9. To obtain more information about "Values in Action," write to People Wise Publications, 14252 East Mall, Irvine, California 92714 or call 714-551-6690.

10. Edward Pauly, *The Classroom Crucible* (New York: Basic Books, 1991), 31.

11. To join the Association of American Educators write to AAE, 26012 Marguerite Parkway, #333, Mission Viejo, California 92692.

Chapter 17. Breaking the Orphanage Syndrome: A Paradigm Shift

1. Brigitte Berger and Peter Berger, *The War Over the Family* (Garden City, N.Y.: Anchor Press/Doubleday, 1984), 213.

2. Ibid., 208–9.

3. Cheryl L. Fagnano and Beverly Z. Werber, eds., School, *Family and Community Interaction* (Boulder, Colo.: Westview Press, 1994), 24.

4. Ibid., 45.

Chapter 18. Becoming a Relevant Parent

1. Pauly, *The Classroom Crucible*, 181–85.

Selected Bibliography

Bennett, William J. "The War Over Culture in Education." The Heritage Lectures #341. Washington, D.C.: The Heritage Foundation, 1991.

————. *The De-Valuing of America.* New York: Simon and Schuster, 1992.

Berger, Brigitte, and Peter L. Berger. *The War Over the Family.* Garden City, N.Y.: Anchor Press/Doubleday, 1984.

Carlson, Allan C. *From Cottage to Work Station.* San Francisco: Ignatius Press, 1993.

Duffy, Cathy. *Government Nannies.* Gresham, Ore.: Noble Publishing Associates, 1995.

Fagan, Patrick F. "The Real Root Causes of Violent Crime." Washington, D.C.: A report by the Heritage Foundation, 29 June 1994.

————. "Rising Illegitimacy." A report by the Heritage Foundation, Washington, D.C. 17 March 1995.

Gilder, George. *Wealth and Poverty.* New York: Basic Books, 1981.

Greenberg, David. *The Construction of Homosexuality.* Chicago: University of Chicago, 1988.

Hanusheck, Eric A. *Making Schools Work.* Washington, D.C.: Brookings Institution, 1994.

Kramer, Rita. *Ed School Follies.* New York: Free Press, 1991.

LaBarbera, Peter. "Gay Youth Suicide: Myth Is Used to Promote Homosexual Agenda." Washington, D.C.: Family Research Council, 1994.

Lieberman, Myron. *Public Education: An Autopsy.* Cambridge, Mass.: Harvard University, 1993.

Pauly, Edward. *The Classroom Crucible.* New York: BasicBooks, 1991.

Spring, Joel. *The American School 1642–1985.* Whiteplains, N.Y.: Longman, 1986.

Stanton, Glenn T. "The Social Significance of the Traditional Two-Parent Family." Colorado Springs: Focus on the Family Public Policy Division, January 1995.

Sykes, Charles J. *A Nation of Victims.* New York: St. Martin's, 1992.

Vitz, Paul C. *Censorship: Evidence of Bias in Our Children's Textbooks.* Ann Arbor, Mich.: Servant, 1986.

Index